Dancing the Wave

Dancing

Audacity, Equilibrium, and Other Mysteries of

the Wave

Surfing

Jean–Étienne Poirier

Translated by Michael H. Kohn

Shambhala
Boston & London
2003

Shambhala Publications, Inc.
Horticultural Hall
300 Massachusetts Avenue
Boston, Massachusetts 02115
www.shambhala.com

© 2000 Les Editions du Septentrion
1300, avenue Maguire
Sillery, Quebec G1T 1Z3
Canada
Originally published in French under the title *Hopupu*.

Translation copyright © 2003 by Shambhala Publications

Printed in the United States of America

∞ This edition is printed on acid-free paper that meets the
American National Standards Institute z39.48 Standard.
♻ Shambhala Publications makes every effort to print on recycled paper.
For more information please visit www.shambhala.com.

Distributed in the United States by Random House, Inc., and
in Canada by Random House of Canada Ltd

Library of Congress Cataloging-in-Publication Data
Poirier, Jean-Étienne, 1973–
[*Hopupu*. English]
Dancing the wave: audacity, equilibrium, and other mysteries of surfing/
Jean-Étienne Poirier: translated by Michael H. Kohn.—1st Shambhala ed.
p. cm.
ISBN 978-1-59030-060-2 (pbk.)
1. Surfing. 2. Human ecology. 3. Surfers—Anecdotes. I. Title.
GV840.S8P57 2003
797.3'2—dc21
2003042518

Ho•pu•pu *n* (Hawaiian): sublime state experienced by a person who has just become one with a wave—ecstasy.

Contents

Dancing the Wave

Introduction

Only the ephemeral has a lasting place.
—Anonymous graffiti

*B*alance. It is what brings about success in love as well as in a tightrope act; it is as fundamental to philosophy as it is to science. It makes our planet Earth dance in the galaxy; or looking closer in, it is that which, if we cry too much, makes us laugh, and also laugh until we cry.

The still, pivotal point of being and the universe, equilibrium is what brings about the moment of stillness and thereby at the same time defines movement and change, the only thing in our lives that can be said to be constant.

From harmony to the state of rest, from calmness and communion to fullness and serenity, there seem to be many advantages to living in a balanced universe. It's like this: if two elements that are in the process of finding equilibrium exchange and share their differences, eliminating whatever makes the scale tip to one side, they give up some of their individual qualities, do away with a relationship of domination, and refuse to get stuck in a condition that is distorted and unjust. In this sense balance is a letting go of identity, perhaps a step toward freedom.

If there is one concept that sums up the challenge that faces humanity in the new millennium, it is balance—the balance that gives us peace instead of war, the balance between consumption and respect for the precious resources of the earth.

The kind of balance that interests me is the kind that human beings experience between themselves and the environment. My wish is to show a manifestation of balance that can be realized in perfect complicity with the sometimes mysterious forces that seem to rule the elements of nature.

Surfing can provide a harmonious and artistic example of the intimate link between Homo sapiens and these real but invisible forces. It can provide proof that this animal can understand the power of the sun, the energy that awakens, the ultimate fire, the circle of intense life. My first objective in writing, then, is to stimulate creativity, to encourage reflection, but it is also to recall the refreshment and satisfaction that is found in the simplicity of the accomplished act. This little book, above and beyond its involvement with the world of surfing, aspires to be a tool that will permit travel in a universe where, for brief moments, this freedom we long for so much can become more than merely a dream.

There are many activities that make it possible for us to engage in what I'll call riding and experience its delights. It might be downhill or cross-country skiing, hang gliding, or parachute jumping. I have chosen surfing because it seems to me to be the ultimate metaphor: a true poetry of harmony, staggering in the relationship it sets up between the immensity of the scene and the smallness of the actor within it; somehow disturbing because of the ancientness of our origins and at the same time our *nowness;* ultimately making of us an image of the future.

Riding is action and movement, but first of all it is a moment, a doorway into the space of time where the person, once having abandoned him- or herself to it, has no choice but to engage in the present moment. The moment of tasting this juicy experience is natural to the conscious being—it is the sensation of being alive.

Surfing is an activity that anybody can watch, either on a beach or on television. Surfing in the sense of "free riding" can be experienced by anyone because the water is not the only place one can ride. Passing from one state to another, continuous movement desired or imposed—riding is the art of edging your way in, entering, slipping into the flow.

A surfer is not just someone who owns a board and polishes it because he or she loves it and it helps to define his or her identity. The surfer is first and foremost a human being who is really alive . . . because riding is essentially feeling yourself animated by the force that feeds the wind, existing at the limits of space and time. To ride free, surfers have to be in a state of attunement, engaged, and at the same time, detached.

Still living in a privileged relationship to the elements of nature but caught fast in modernity by the bonds of commerce that bind them to an entire industry that is devoted to them, surfers live on the borderline between two paradoxical worlds: they are trying simply to be, but at the same time they often live on their image alone, feeding on recognition that is based purely on appearances.

They are a social enigma, a dynamic example of human beings who are looking for fundamental balance at a moment in history that sometimes seems to be massively cultivating inertia.

Acting in the midst of dissipations of energy that manage to keep a part of their mysteries hidden from the masterminds of physics, surfers themselves form a part of the archetype of modern mysticism.

In Quebec, though we are far from being immersed in a world of palm trees, it is not hard to observe many activities that have surfing as their ancestor—snowboarding and skateboarding, for example. Not a single week passes without our being presented with some image from surfing or some reference to it in advertising. From what the commercials tell us, it is no longer necessary to get your feet wet to surf: people "surf" on the Internet seated comfortably in their cozy office chairs.

Surfing is big. At least on a superficial level it is pervasive; yet in point of fact it is not easy to get at the root of this notion—the free riding of the surfer and its history—the simple visual presentation of which evokes all its richness and power. This is why I have decided to enter, as by osmosis, through the doorway of surfing into a discussion aimed at attempting to convey the ineffable, to recall to mind the experience of *hopupu*.

1 | Wanderings of a Gremmie

Enjoying life and wandering—these are the two poles for
those who are supposed to develop culture.
—Michel Maffesoli

*F*ar be it from me to tell you about my feats and exploits, because
my journey is that of an amateur, of an anthropologist who has
skipped out of the library in order to read reality with his heart. My
wish is to bear witness to things that have emerged within me and
remained. Moreover, all through this book, I will have little to say
about the competitions and athletic feats that have marked the history of surfing. In this chapter, I will be presenting to you the essence
of a few journeys I took, events I experienced on a gut level, the very
moments that led me to envy those wild youths, surfers and apostles
of the wind, and to travel along with them.

These brief anecdotes, which describe my journey into the universe of riding, seek both to be entertaining and to provide a sense
of the initiation, as well as to allow the reader to take the plunge into
a state of mind that is favorable to understanding feeling and emotion, a state of mind that is open to the impalpable. Because several
aspects of surfing can be perceived only by means of union with the
senses, these few pages have the function of awakening or bringing
to life the sense receptors, quietly, one by one, before moving on to
make a deeper, more integral call on our being, leading to the point
where a sense of movement and balance begin to emerge from the
process.

Though subtle to begin with, the call of the sea can become completely intoxicating, a mad drunkenness for those who surf day and night. You become obsessed with it because it enables you to find your center, the still point you pivot around. You will live hand-to-mouth in order to make progress and launch yourself into orbit. It hypnotizes you because it is rhythmic and tireless. Yes, the temptations of the sea are great and desirable. Far from being the mere sum of simple elements in the periodic table, the sea is a source of existence, a magnetic, 360-degree world in which being grows larger; for a sea voyage begins with seduction, then transforms and unifies life and death.

It is a matter of engagement, planting your foot in a universe that is overlooked today—or forgotten—the universe of nature as a mystery, a realm frequently effaced from existence. So in order to give my readers an idea of a similar experience without forcing them to dip their toes themselves (that is, make a timid advance on the beach, board under arm), I am going to recount a portion of my own journey. Though just one among an infinitude of waves, it is the one that I felt with my own body and saw with my own eyes; therefore, it is the one I can talk about with the most truth and intensity. These are facts based in experience, real stories, and therefore, at the very least, possible.

The First Sideskids

As with any other North American bombarded by journalistic reports, news, and advertisements, it wasn't just yesterday that I first took in the image of one of my fellow beings at work on the face of a wave, though the idea of actually getting myself into that situation took a long time to ripen. Ironically, it was in the course of an ice-climbing trip that it came to me for the first time.

Frozen water and warm salty water are a world apart. Therefore it took about three years after a climbing friend had pointed out to me how exotic and thrilling surfing would be for climbers and lovers of the cold like us that I finally got it into my head to trade in my ice axes and crampons for something new that would eventually lead me toward the sea: a snowboard.

This was a completely revitalizing discovery, a contact with speed and gravity such as I had never experienced before. It was all about the sensation of the ride rather than practicing a sport. It was an inner quest that was sensually guided by the mother of all reality, the energy that sustains life. I replayed this first mad season of snowboarding with friends of mine, hoping to find out if I was exaggerating when I said that carving the snow on a snowboard could be the height of pleasure. Only a few young women were willing to talk to me about it candidly, and they readily admitted that they had been on the edge of emotions that definitely belonged in the orgasmic range.

Egged on by the ecstasy this revelation aroused in me, I threw myself without hesitation on any device that allowed me to ride without fear, spurred on by new sensations. One evening, intoxicated by the twilight and on my way home by the only means of locomotion I owned (on foot), I stopped at a shop owned by some friends. These friends had invested in the business of selling boards destined for three surfaces that shine when the sun reflects upon them: water, snow, and asphalt. Winter was coming to an end, so it took little time to convince myself to go ahead and acquire a skateboard. I spent a good part of the night working marks into the thin carpet at my house, since the streets still had a fair amount of snow on them.

Inspired by the brand name of my new board, Toy Machine, I left the family nest so I could really be free to play and evolve. Not that my family limited me, but the rug in the house was soon out of bounds, and the battered asphalt in the neighborhood was not as promising as the pavement in the neighborhood of the apartment building I was planning to move to. The apartment in question was located close to the only skateboarding ramp available in my town at that time, a spine-type half-pipe about two meters (six and a half feet) high. This was where I lived while my interest in riding turned into a definite thing. I went to the ramp nearly every day, organizing my work schedule and everything else around my daily training sessions.

My learning period in skateboarding, punctuated by painful falls at the bottom of the ramp, was less delicious than my beginnings on the snowboard. All in all, it amounted more or less to a succession of painful incidents that came to a head when my right hip, my favored landing point when I fell from the heights of the metal wave, became so bruised that I had to walk for a few days with a cane.

Taunted and incited by all those young people around me (described by some as sluggish and lazy, but from where I was, they were fairly exploding into the air), I continued on with my training, though not without tearful moments. It was not until after a whole summer of practice that I was able to surf the ramp with ease and control and to dodge small obstacles as I moved about in town. A more aerial approach to riding and one less forgiving for beginners than any other, skateboarding was, no contest, the most rigorous discipline I had ever faced.

It took me another summer to be able to do turns on the ramp in a fluid manner and to try the kinds of maneuvers that proved to be just as rich in sensations as those on the snowboard had been. The warm sun working on the muscles of my back provided me with joyful compensation for the extra effort that had to be put in. And on top of that, there are certain states of the soul that are available only in the summertime.

In the meantime, I was given another board, which proved itself a good substitute for real surfing: a longboard. This is a type of skateboard that is usually somewhere in the area of a meter (three feet) long and flexible in a way that makes you feel as though the board were dipping below ground level when you are doing turns, thereby providing the simple but so-exciting sensation of carving waves. When you combine the freedom of placing yourself on the board with the extraordinary speeds you can attain with the longboard's big wheels, the resulting way of evolving in space turns out to be simply too brilliant for me to describe in the restrictive medium of words. Let us just say that a harmony between mind and body occurs that causes the rider to develop a profound sense of grace and balance, to get high on the happiness of moving in space, with the body expressing the sweetness of the moment without having to furnish the slightest effort toward propulsion. Floating!

Since my patience has the virtue of being limited, it was not long before I organized the first trip to go surfing in the ocean. Steve, a friend from work, and Yans, the owner of that evil shop that kept remodeling my destiny, joined me in the adventure, since they too had the urge to get into the waves and take a few days of vacation.

One Mouthful at a Time

We chose our destination by the name of the town, an evocative name for would-be surfers if there ever was one: Surf City. Located on Long Beach Island, New Jersey, this town is made up of a garland of little houses built on pilings. Surfing shops filled with boards of all shapes and sizes, seductive visions of beaches, and images of bodies each one more athletic than the next fed our desire to become surfers too.

We quickly began the search that led to the purchase of our boards, a process that involved going into a small shop by the name of Brighton Beach Surf Shop. The shop was owned by a surfing legend, if we were to judge by the period photographs in which the owner appeared in the splendor of his youth, carrying on one arm a goddess of a woman as he hurtled down a wave of foam, his eyes gleaming with the flame of passion. His son, who was as privileged a physical specimen as his father, imparted judicious advice. He took care to guide us with the greatest patience we ever experienced anywhere in this sort of place, where the respect you get, it seems, usually derives from your reputation as a surfer.

Despite the modest dimensions of the shop's inventory, our respect was appropriately large, given the spirit that emanated from the owner's whole family around the objects of our lust. The photographs of the young man, who was a surfing instructor and a shaper, also helped to inspire a sense of reverence and awe in us. One of these photos showed the total audacity the dude was capable of: it immortalized him as a child in a highly stylized moment as he was executing a skateboard jump off the roof of a garage. A variety of more recent photos documented his talents as a surfer, while another, also

dating from his childhood, showed the rebel he must have been in those days; he was executing a radical move in the air over the hood of a police car. A visit to the hangar that sheltered the family's collection of about a hundred boards, one of which had to be at least six meters (twenty feet) long,¹ completed the tour. We were deeply impressed.

After receiving advice on stickers from the patriarch, we went outside to chat a little more with his son and get directions to the beach. Having moved three used boards, he could now consider his selling day over.

Oddly enough, he had never seen a longboard skateboard. He eagerly grabbed one of ours and executed a few turns before our bedazzled eyes. He was as supple as a spring, ready to explode with force as he performed some short-radius turns punctuated with flowing, controlled sideskids. The board was a skillful piece of work, the product of an enterprise out of California by the name of Sector 9. Here its possibilities were being shown to best advantage. Without a doubt, this guy had a clear awareness of communion between the spirit, the body, and matter.

Overwhelmed, dazed by the sun, our minds ravished by his exhibition, we left looking for a place to spend the night. The owner sealed the moment with a traditional and picturesque "hang loose" gesture. Pure movement.

Our lodging turned out to be the outdoor area behind a superstore, whose vast, sloping parking lot allowed us to work off some of our excess excitement, which was fueled by large amounts of refreshments.

At dawn we started on our way to the sea, the destination we had been longing for. There, our first moments were essentially spent getting used to handling the boards, which were astonishingly light and fragile. All day long we participated in a perpetual repetition. The waves don't pause to allow surfers to move forward, so we worked on getting the hang of the basic techniques of navigating on a surfboard. The first stage is to learn to get past the incoming waves so that you can finally reach the lineup, which is just beyond where the waves start to break.

Lying on my board, a vivid, metallic-flake orange Gordon & Smith from the 1980s, I spent a long time being pushed back, capsized, and carried away by the waves before I mastered the skill of tipping the front end of the board into the face of the wave in order to get past.

The salt water running from my hair into my mouth, stirring up a feeling akin to irritation but still gentle and motivating; my shoulders constantly called upon for the work of paddling; my pride hidden away in the deepest part of me, I did my best to immerse myself in the moment. Little by little, my reading of the waves improved and I succeeded in getting past the turbulent zone to where I could see the future waves, cresting like small undulating cliffs, as I sat peacefully astride my foamy mount, in balance on it for the first time. It was a magical moment, a terrifically relaxing one, in which the ocean rocked me as I waited for the wave that was destined for me.

Life not often being as convenient as dreams, it took me the whole day and a change of beaches before I was able to stand up on a wave. I was far from being able to try any kind of special maneuver, but I was still surprised by my unexpected success at the end of a day that I had spent essentially absorbing a phenomenal amount of seawater. I was happy enough to raise my arms and shout, victorious in my own eyes but idiotic to the numerous sun worshipers relaxing on the beach.

The same experience of being able to stand up was repeated in the days that followed without my really having the time to understand exactly how it happened. And each time, I raised my fists to the sky against my better intentions and in spite of the conditioning I had imposed on myself by practicing on the skateboard and the visualizations I had in my head from all the surfing films I had managed to get my hands on. The result? Nose first into the water. I immediately suffered the consequences of an act I actually wanted no part of. This made me look like quite an idiot. All the same, the spirit of surfing was being instilled into my companions and me, one mouthful of salt water at a time.

Ocean City, the second place we visited in the course of our first trip, during which the names of the towns seemed to show us the route to follow, allowed us to advance a bit further in our sea training. There we met a friendly shop manager who one evening insisted on our accepting a place to sleep when he learned that I was buying a knit cap at his store because I was going to have to spend the night beneath the stars.

The evening—passed in the company of individuals who had remained stuck in the oral stage of their development—was worthy of the highest praise given the circumstances: boredom in one of the shabbiest places in existence. But by contrast the wake-up was one of true adventure—guided by the moment, improvised, and quickly directed to action. Stretched out between two aisles in the store, where we had passed the night, providing an unusual spectacle to the passersby who pressed their faces against the glass, I awoke to the sound of the shop owner tuning a radio to the weather report.

After a moment of intent listening, he shouted at the top of his lungs, as though we were miles away, "Hey, guys, grab your boards, the waves are coming!" Two stages, a thousand movements: we simply crossed the street and began surfing with a really talented guy who knew how to take maximum advantage of the elements. I managed to stand up only one more time and got rather frustrated watching this brute moving back and forth again and again on the waves while the rest of us were busy trying to achieve a balance between the liquid we had taken into our stomachs and that of the surrounding waters. Over and over he appeared, standing up on his board on the cascading, driving stuff that for us was just so much evanescence and foam. This man impressed me with his ability to extract from nature a joy that was difficult for me to grasp but seemed somehow freely within my reach.

After this we had a brief but stimulating conversation with the champ. He was like an oracle revealing to me the simple intensity and love a man can feel for surfing. I traded T-shirts with my spiritual guide of the moment, and after a hearty lunch, we were called on to other places.

In athletic terms, the adventure concluded with a memorable session in an outdoor skateboarding park. The newly initiated (to the longboard) locals showed us the reverence normally reserved for "old school" veterans of the sport. It was really the surfboards on the roof of our car and the fact that I was handing out stickers from a magazine I was editing at the time and some from Yans's shop that really brought us the status. Yans and I also owed a great part of the glory we blithely enjoyed to Steve, thanks to the splendid rail slides he performed repeatedly to the admiration of all. After talking with the local heroes and offering some vague advice, we took our leave of this place, now marked forever by the passage of the three "wise men."

Resolved to continue our surfing, we drove a good part of the night looking for an affordable motel. This was truly a downer. The most miserable hovels, drawn from the macabre vision of Stephen King were priced at no less than fifty dollars a night. As the road wore on and on, our pleasure in the whole escapade totally petered out.

The culmination of our bargaining adventures was a negotiation that was worth experiencing despite the pain of this part of the trip. We went into a kind of hangar that had the look and feel of an auto body repair shop, and there we found ourselves in the presence of an old man who sat facing a television set hanging from a suspension arm. He looked at us in the TV screen as though it were a mirror. Without losing a bit of his intense absorption in the program he was watching, he greeted us with a kind of snort.

> "Hmm?"
> "Do you have a room for two?" (Steve liked to sleep on the
> floor.)
> "Yes."
> "And how much is it?"
> "Seventy dollars."
> "Seventy American dollars!?" I exclaimed, completely stu-
> pefied.

And then the old man, for all the world like a cow laboring to produce a sound, turned to us, revealing his hideous countenance, and added "Plus taaaaax!"

I'd always thought of the U.S. as the place where you could buy anything—whatever you wanted—and usually from a friendly person who was happy to make the sale. So, to come across an American who was openly hostile while offering patently bad accommodations for an outrageous price was a real cultural shock.

Things appeared to improve when we reached a very nice little marina that seemed well qualified as a vagrant sleeping facility. But a storm broke out and Yans and I were forced to sleep in the car, which rapidly turned into a putrid sauna, the result of closed windows and damp wetsuits. Steve sheltered comfortably (to all appearances) in a strange little cabin that housed the marina's public toilets. In the morning, disgusted by the torrid and smelly night, we didn't have the energy to surf in the storm and we departed for home, without even taking the time to express our appreciation to the inhabitants of that lost corner of the world for their hospitality.

Viva Mexico, Cabrones!

It was during a surfing trip to Mexico that I realized it would be to my great advantage to spend more time trying to understand the dynamics of waves rather than just trying to reach a standing position on the board at any price. The size and rhythm of the breaking waves demanded prudence. I had to accept the evidence that the secret of surfing was being able to evaluate properly the amplitude, rhythm, and energy of the wave coming to meet you.

This observation regarding patience took noble oratorical form in the mouth of the Mexican who was renting me a board emblazoned with the Jamaican flag. He looked hard at me, taking in my excited state, and very simply said, "Hey, man, take it easy." I took the road to the beach mentally repeating this adage: "Man, if you want to surf here, take it easy." This phrase resounded in my head like a mantra while a passionate desire for salt water began welling up within me. It had been more than six months since I had come in contact with seawater.

Evaluate, paddle at top speed, evaluate again, and then position your board at the angle that exposes the greatest amount of its surface to the water that is rolling toward the beach. Gauge the size of the waves that are there right now and try to keep a cool head. I had thought a long time about how to reach a standing position on the board, the moment that grabs you when you are watching films, but I hadn't taken the time to visualize how to "capture" the force of the wave.

If at Surf City I had had beginner's luck, at Puerto Escondido, in the Mexican Pipeline,[2] I caught glimpses into multicolored tubes that were forming right near me, a challenge to be conquered. These were tubes of close to two meters (about six feet) that took form very quickly and had a very thin lip—fine envelopes of water that came and isolated the surfer from the universe for a period of a few seconds, the time needed to be reborn, to carve the wave within.

Several times, on my knees or with feet firmly planted on my board, I hurtled down the shoulder of one of these huge waves and had the intimidating experience of feeling the draft coming off the tube as it took shape, and I had the good fortune to catch sight of the rainbow forming on its crest. Only once did I manage to stand up completely. Taunted by François, a more experienced friend who gave me the bogus advice to cut down deeper and deeper, I kept positioning myself too far forward on the board, and it was often head over heels that I ended my attempts at conquest. The one time I managed to get completely to a standing position, I was still too far forward and instead of shooting down the face of the wave, I started surfing directly on top of it, on top of the forming tube. It was surely the fear of being pushed forward headfirst that enabled me to get "air" (for the first and last time that day). I landed in front of the wave, stunning my tyrannical companion, who up to that point thought he was going to carry off the day's honors. I took advantage of this moment of glory to get out of the water, very happy to hang on to the thought of this glorious feat as the highlight of the day.

Never did Mexican tortas seem so delicious. I allowed myself two of them. This dish was an enormous round sandwich that cost a dollar, garnished with avocados, onions, and tomatoes. Freshly caught tuna contributed to the delicious meal, and the whole was washed down nicely with a couple of beers at a few pennies apiece. The adventure, the pure air, and the good, healthy food—these were a few of the ingredients that I came to understand as making up the surfer's daily life. What emerged as the most strongly imprinted memory, indeed the most convincing one, was having seen and felt the call of the pipeline, the tube, a translucent and luminous space, a tunnel that drew you into a multisensory experience.

Somewhat bored—and frankly irritated—by watching the pros tirelessly describing curves in the waves, we sat on the beach feeling like losers. Surrounded by lovely women who ignored us (they were watching the men in the water) and unable to keep up in the surf, we felt like kids at an adult party—left out and invisible. We left Mexico full of excitement about the news I'd received from my brother: a half meter of powder had just fallen in Quebec. We took our revenge among the white waves.

Journey to Maine

Yans and I now owned our own surfboards, and looking at them set up like totem poles against the walls of our rooms kept our memories alive. We had had some actual surfing experience, and the sea was again calling to us. One fine day, at five in the morning, about the time I was returning home from some amusement or another, Yans picked me up at the house and we hurried toward what seemed to be the most reachable destination: Wells Beach, in the state of Maine.

The first day, this beach provided very little in the way of satisfaction—frigid water and nothing but small-time rollers. Putting that aside, though, the cabin we'd rented was quite comfortable and the streets were well suited for our longboard junkets. All the same, we had come to surf, and after passing the time for a while in this mysteriously muffled and foggy atmosphere, we began prospecting and eventually found a surfing spot whose name I do not precisely recall, but I know how to get there. I found it again later on, as though by instinct.

Since access to the site was via a paid parking lot, we looked for a gap in the defenses that would allow us to get to the sea for free, saving us the many dollars that the soldiers of capitalism, bunkered in their tollbooth, were demanding. A little farther along, the grounds of a luxury hotel gave onto the beaches where the best waves were coming in. After having donned our neoprene wetsuits (and offered to passersby the spectacle of our nudity), we entered the gardens of the hotel, boards under our arms. Assuming our most haughty mien, raising our chins to the horizon in a gesture that was meant to be full of confidence, we succeeded in crossing this area as though it belonged to us. At just the moment we were beginning to think we had pulled off a very easy maneuver, we came to the fence that we would have to get past to reach the beach. As a security measure, the gate was padlocked on both sides. That is to say, we would need a key to get off the grounds we were so courageously invading. Caught in a trap but still on the alert, I simulated searching for a fictitious key inside my suit as a woman, returning to the gilded realm, kindly opened the door for me, almost as though she were embarrassed for not having acted sooner. With smiles splitting our faces from ear to ear, it took us hardly a moment to lose ourselves in the water and continue on with our apprenticeship. Since the waves were small, this was the perfect occasion for a detailed study.

With the almost ten dollars we saved on parking, plus an additional five apiece, we refreshed ourselves at a lobster stand. The lobsters were very good but still far from as tasty as the ones from the Gulf of Saint Lawrence, better nourished as they are in an environment of organic wastes.

Back at the cabin, I decided to risk my first session of night surfing, guided by a moon that reliably prevents me from sleeping when it gets anywhere near full. The silence, broken only by the sound of the waves, filled and stimulated me yet also reminded me that I was not very visible in the dark and was also blocked from view by the sprays of water blown up by the wind. Yans, watching me from the beach, comfortably seated and rhythmically bathed by the waves in the shallows, looked to me like a mirage. It felt as though he were a teacher whose presence alone was encouraging my efforts.

That did it for me. We had reconnected with the spirit of what had seduced us the summer before. We returned home with the feeling of not having pacified but rather further fed our need to surf.

On the way home, the call of the road was strong, and I visited New Brunswick for the first time in my life and the Chaleurs Bay. We arrived in Percé with the rising sun, with Yans at the wheel. We had put hundreds of kilometers behind us in a twenty-four hour period. It was an adventure in which the countryside going by constituted the main enjoyment. Ending at the entrance to Forillon National Park, on the Gaspé Peninsula of northern Quebec, this trip had been a long meditation.

The Utopian Wave

Before my very first surfing trip, I had been traveling around the Gaspé Peninsula for a few weeks, without any intention other than seeing the sea and, if wishes could come true, hearing the song of a few sirens. In brief, I was in search of something intangible. The upshot was an encounter with neither more nor less than one siren and a wave that was perfect for surfing.

Was it chance, destiny, or chaos? It all depends on your view of the interdependence of events. In any case, I had the opportunity to see the sea at Cape Rosiers being driven by a titanic fury, a rare thing in the summertime. This was the result of the same bad weather that had caused a serious flood in the region of Lake Saint John. The waves that came up even impressed the locals. I, who thought that this was just the normal thing, was overjoyed to say to myself that there was nothing equal to the surf of my own native land. When I got home I alerted everyone to the situation. Incredulous, many surfers dismissed my report as unrealistic ranting.

So I went back a year later (after having been initiated) and discovered that surfing waves were, indeed, rare. All the same, I discovered another very beautiful surfing spot, the exact location of which shall remain a mystery to my readers. It provided me with a precious moment, somewhere between a dream and a hallucination. One session, permeated by a supernatural atmosphere in which the entire sky seemed to be blanketed by a single cloud pierced by a few potent rays of sunlight, set off in me a whirlwind of speculation concerning the deviant fantasies of those in possession of nuclear arms. On a more physical level, there was this beautiful swell, splendidly slow, which brought me a visitor in the form of a gray seal of close to three hundred kilograms (more than six hundred pounds). Although unquestionably less frightening than a shark, the beast, too curious for my taste, seemed intent on letting me know he was a more legitimate resident of those parts than I was and convinced me to calmly return to the beach. In any case, the experience made clear that it is not only surfers who practice territoriality when the good waves are up.

On this trip I also visited the Magdalen Islands. I surfed there a little bit, but apparently the time to go is in the fall, especially to the beach at Martinique, where I had the good fortune to enjoy a few waves. Though it's not quite a microcosm of Hawaii on Quebec soil, I do have a good memory of the place in the season that precedes winter, a period of dramatic changes that often lead to storms. The Bay of Fundy, Newfoundland, and Nova Scotia seem to be equally rich in good places to surf. When I am on the East Coast, I will return to these places, I will see again what is there, and I will surf!

Trip to Boston

I invested a lot of hope in a trip to Boston, the result of a promise I had made to myself during the first hours of my novitiate in surfing: My plan was to reach a certain level of competence within a respectable period of time, clearly and unmistakably, so that I would not see my inspiration dissipate like a dream with the first rays of morning. How much time would I allow myself? The time it took for my hair, which was rather short at the time, to reach my shoulders. This agenda appealed to me as one that cannot be ignored, that is natural, and that is effective by virtue of its relentless presence. I found a partner to join me in accomplishing this mission, a guy in his forties who was more energetic than most of the teenagers I knew. He was equipped with a formidable measure of daring as well as the thirst for discovery necessary for vigilance in the quest for the pleasures of living amid extraordinary challenges.

Bertrand proved his level of interest by immediately buying a neoprene wetsuit and proposing a destination. After borrowing Steve's board, he picked me up in his Jeep, and we headed in the direction of Boston. There we found excellent jazz music and great food at the house of a friend of Bertrand's, who put us up. But as far as the waves were concerned . . . it was the void—a dead-flat horizon without the slightest hint of undulation, the very image that Zen practitioners look for when they want to calm their minds. All the same, I must say this visit to Boston was marked by a stimulating experience, or to be more precise, an experience that was just plain disturbing.

The whole thing started at a parachuting facility. Bertrand himself was a veteran parachutist, and he was telling me about the sport's virtues as we were watching a young woman landing in a field. It seemed as if she hit the ground and departed from the scene as quickly as she had jumped from the airplane—unfortunately, in the direction of the hospital. That very evening we saw a video of another accident taken by a parachuting enthusiast who had been with us that day. The poor jumper apparently had been trying to pull off a spectacular landing maneuver and had lost his bearings. He crashed into a sheet metal structure of some kind, cutting his knee and banging his head. He immediately lost the use of one eye. Feeling far from enthusiastic about the more exciting aspects of skydiving, I reflected on the dangers of all activities that have a risky side, including surfing, as we will see later.

These sad thoughts of danger evaporated while surfing the following day, when I executed my first real turn and had my first long ride. I had time to feel the acceleration, to adjust my pressure on the board, to take on speed, and to become intoxicated with flying on water. I plunged into the water headfirst at the end of my mad dash, with all the elegance that can come from happiness. I came up smiling in a postorgasmic state, convinced that death has no meaning if one has not fully tasted life and that the risks were up to a certain point unavoidable, but so were the joys. I also clearly realized that when you opt for action, you choose to live fully, and from this perspective each little action is perceived as a declaration that affirms your condition as a living being. I later ran across the remarks of Louis-Vincent Thomas, who points out in the introduction to his work on fantasies that "man only affirms himself in and through action, successively manipulating and transforming matter, changing his location in space, domesticating time."[3]

But enough of this philosophizing, let us return to the account of our adventure. We were now at the famous surfing spot where I had gone with Yans, near Wells Beach, Maine. Bertrand and I ended up there by coming up the coast from the south, studying the waves as we drove along. I had never done this before, doubtless owing to my instinctive approach. I have to say that in any case, whether you come slowly up the coast or not, at some point you end up at *that* spot; that is where the waves are, and that is what surfers are looking for. This time we paid for the parking and we had a very full day, standing up on our boards as I had never had the chance to do before with a friend, crossing each other in the waves, exchanging grins, shouting to the elements warriors' cries of pleasure.

I was happy because I had accomplished my mission and met my challenge. I could cut my hair because that day I had caught more waves than I had on any of my previous trips. As for Bertrand, though he did not suggest that he was thinking about permanently hanging up his parachute, he had unquestionably discovered a new way to externalize his love of life and nature.

We returned home on Sunday, tearing along a road littered by moose, a mink, a fox, and a few illusions. I was awakened by Bertrand on Monday morning. Our Boston host, who had gone parachute jumping the day we had our memorable escapade on the surf, was the sole survivor of a terrible plane crash that had killed one of his roommates and three other friends. So ends our reflection on life and death.

The Quest

With these adventures at an end, I was now fully engaged on a ride that I hoped would always continue to make me more spontaneous and freer from rational barriers—always more open to an understanding of the music of nature calling to me.

What follows is the history of this urge, this imperative, that is shared by a considerable portion of humanity. It is an account of an ever growing number of people who follow in the footprints of the first surfers, the Polynesians. We wander lost with regard to social norms and modernity, continually searching for an echo of truth in a revived relationship with nature. Aloha!

2 | Some History

*T*o attempt to travel back to the first moments of surfing is to voyage to a past where there are no official reference points. Surfing, or originally *he'e nalu* in ancient Hawaiian, is an aquatic practice, the first appearance of which is impossible to date with any precision. Because the Polynesians didn't keep written records, historians don't have evidence of the birthdate of surfing. The collective memory of the first populations that practiced surfing was, however, preserved through certain chants, *meles* in Hawaiian. The presumed date of the beginnings of surfing varies depending on the source, but was likely sometime around 1500 B.C.E. What is incontestable is that the practice of surfing has survived until the present, carrying along a rich heritage whose dominant values are striking in their relevance to our world today—respect for the earth, the celebration of the pure joy of living, and a quest for an ever more refined sense of balance in space.

Prehistory

In attempting to reconstruct the origin of surfing, one discovers certain artifacts that can still be observed in the places where surfing is practiced. These are canoes and other forms of seacraft, with or without sails, invented in the Pacific by the first human beings who dared to leave the Eurasian continent. It was probably these modest devices that made it possible to discover the pleasure of riding the surf.

Those who conceived and constructed these floating vehicles were the ancestors of the Polynesian community of our time. Their forebears were themselves the descendents of a mixture of Caucasian and Mongolian groups who, moving toward the east of Eurasia, scattered throughout a region now known as Melanesia. They were driven on in their movements by a purpose of which nothing is any longer known.

This first migration into the immensity of the ocean, which took place in an area of many islands, permitted the basic development of an art of navigation that was to become a historic model. These people's relationship with nature is clearly shown in the construction of their catamarans and canoes in paintings, in historic documents, and in reconstructions. It can be seen in the design of their sails and hulls as well as in their ingenious use of simple raw materials—hollowed logs, woven coconut fibers, and a variety of long leaves. The whole thing is simply amazing. The craftsmanship is so precise that it makes you wonder if the Polynesians were the beneficiaries of extraterrestrial revelations, as people frequently like to imagine with regard to other civilizations of this period that erected monuments whose engineering remains astonishing in the present day.

After a few generations of accumulated navigational experience in the direction of Indonesia, these people developed an expertise for seafaring that subsequently opened the entire Pacific to human occupation. Equipped with a lunar calendar and guided by the signs in the sky, the movements of fishing birds, and the maritime currents, the Polynesians first landed on the Bismarck Archipelago, located to the northeast of New Guinea. Between 1500 and 1000 B.C.E., they arrived in Tonga, Fiji, and Samoa. It is around this time that the Polynesians seem to have lost contact with the islands to the west and that we see the beginnings of a culturally distinct civilization.

Approximately another millennium was to pass before the Polynesians carried out another migration. Around 300 B.C.E. they made an epic voyage of about three thousand kilometers (more than eighteen hundred miles) in the face of powerful winds and currents, their canoes loaded down with plants, animals, and people. Their firm intention was to find new lands to colonize; and they found them in the region of the Marquesas Islands.

The third and last period of migrations came between 300 B.C.E. and 1000 C.E. These last epic migrations were different from the previous ones in that they do not seem to have been occasioned by demographic pressure or the threats of war but by a pure spirit of adventure.

Return journeys to central Polynesia were undertaken in order to bring back the message of the new territorial discoveries that had been made—among which it should be mentioned were included Easter Island, Tahiti, and then, finally, Hawaii—and arrangements were made for the transport of resources needed for the organization of the colonial effort. The discovery of Hawaii is variously attributed to a Polynesian by the name of Hawaii'iloa and to an individual from Tahiti. Tahiti was the island that was in some way the base camp from which the expeditions that ended up in Hawaii were launched. Reference is also made in this connection to a Maori from New Zealand.

Contact with the Water

The first reason for surfing the waves arose in daily work. The Polynesians had to be able to get past the barrier reefs and back to the shore rapidly. Beyond that, they began relating to the waves in the spirit of pleasure and relaxation. It should be pointed out that the majority of men whose livelihood developed out of the sea during this period were what today are called watermen. In contrast to the priest-navigators who guided the long crossings of the high seas, these people fished mainly along the shores, and it was here that they developed their aptitude for faring on the waves.

The practice of surfing was born mainly out of a relationship with the agitated waters along the coasts of the Pacific islands and within the context of ventures out onto the sea for fishing and other purposes, but its genesis is also linked with the simple act of swimming. To speak of a date for the beginning of swimming would be pure speculation. Nonetheless, John Bloomfield, the editor of a work on swimming and surfing in Australia, proposes going back four thousand years to Egypt to find the traces of the first aquatic sports. Nobody will ever know how the first swimming lesson unfolded. Did it happen when someone fell into the water by accident? Did it happen in an attempt to imitate swimming animals? In any case, swimming is surely one of the first things human beings learned to do in their contact with the ocean. Swimming in the sea, where one's body is liable to be suddenly propelled forward by a wave, remains the purest form of riding the surf.

After having traveled the Pacific and arrived in Hawaii, Polynesians were relieved of the labor of preparing for long voyages and were able to spend more of their time in pursuit of leisure. At that point, the practice of he'e nalu took on a more complete form, and its practitioners began to put into it some of the energy and passion for discovery that they had developed in the course of the long migrations that had marked their history.

From riding the waves while swimming to the practice of surfing in a canoe or with a variety of small boards, the art began to spread in the Pacific. Hawaii remained the focal point of this activity, even though identical practices appeared in other remote places on the planet.

For example, Malcolm Gault-Williams, an ethnologist based in California who specializes in surfing, tells us in the first chapter of his work entitled *Legendary Surfers* that several historians of surfing—including Tom Blake, Ben Finney, and James Houston—have mentioned the existence of the practice of surfing at points on the globe that at the time had no probability of contact with the Hawaiians. They speak of Peru, where ancient pottery has been found illustrating humans surfing on the sea. They also mention Africa, where the British explorer Sir James Edward Alexander observed the practice of surfing in 1835, a scene described in the first and second volumes of his 1837 work, *Alexander's Narrative of a Voyage of Observation among the Colonies of West Africa*.

The Matter of Boards

Wood was most likely the first material used for surfing the waves. Rigid and supple at the same time, wood can be treated with a variety of oils, and it ages with incomparable beauty. It is difficult to imagine what other resource could have been used in remote times to fashion a board suitable for dancing on the sea. Although until recently wood remained the raw material most often used for making surfboards, now it is only the artisans who produce deluxe custom longboards (surf, not skateboard, that is) who are likely to use it.

In Hawaii, the making of a board began with the selection of a tree. The custom was to place a *kumu* (fish) ceremonially at the foot of the chosen tree. The tree, whether it was a *wili wili*, an *ulu*, or a *koa*, was then cut down, and the fish was placed in a hole dug nearby. The stripped trunk was taken to the beach and placed in a shelter used for making canoes and other watercraft. Using tools made of bone or stone, the board was sculpted for a specific use, within the natural limits of the properties of the material. The surfboard was then polished by hand with a stone called *'oahi*, after having been sanded down with coral to smooth the surface and perfect the definition of the curves.

Once the final form had been obtained, the last phase of production consisted in coating it with various mixtures, including oil derived from a nut called *kukui*, the sap of the tree that produced the same nut, the juice of banana flowers, and ashes derived from the burning of certain leaves. The board was sometimes even covered with mud. Whatever ingredients were chosen, the goal was to bring out the grain of the wood and offer some water resistance.

The final product was called in Hawaiian *papa he'e nalu* (board that makes possible becoming one with a wave). We can enumerate four major design types: the *olo*, the *kiko'o*, the *alaia*, and the *paipo*. The specific qualities of these boards are only roughly known, although ancient examples in the Bishop Museum of Honolulu and the Museum of Archaeology and Anthropology of the University of Pennsylvania give an idea of the earliest designs.

The olo, which was a board around six meters (twenty feet) in length, was perfectly adapted for waves that do not form a hollow face, sometimes called sheep. These are patches of bubbling water that do not develop to the point of breaking waves. This was predominately a board for upper-class Hawaiians (*ali'i*),[4] although it could also be used by the working class (*maka'ai-nana*). Lengths of up to seven meters (twenty-three feet) have been reported for this board, which weighed from seventy to eighty kilos (155 to 177 pounds)! Difficult to maneuver, the olo was suited to long straight-line rides rather than the short-radius turns and air maneuvers popular today. When the olo was made of wili wili, it was called an *'owili*. Another name, *'onini*, was used to designate a type of olo that was particularly difficult to surf with and was for this reason reserved for a category of surfers of a very high level.

A close relative of the olo was the kiko'o, which was shorter and for more general use. It seems to have been an evolutionary link between the olo and the alaia, yet unfortunately, the kiko'o is the kind of board about which the least information can be found.

The alaia, which was approximately three meters long (about ten feet), was ideal for what the Hawaiians called the *kakala*: a wave that presents a real challenge because, owing to the depth of its face, it exposes the surfer to a serious risk of death. With a design that is both more convex and thinner (one to three centimeters thick, half an inch to a little over an inch), the alaia is the closest of the old designs to a modern board. Forty-five centimeters wide (about seventeen inches), it was the preferred board of the maka'ai-nana class, although its design was so exceptional that Hawaiians of the ali'i class prized it as well.

The last model, the paipo, is in fact closer to a boogie board than to a surfboard, if you consider it mainly from the point of view of size. It was a meter and twenty-five centimeters long (about four and a half feet) and had a nose (twenty-seven centimeters—eleven inches) wider than its tail (twenty-one centimeters—eight inches).

There is an extant example of one made from wili wili at the University of Pennsylvania. It is convex, with a turned-up tip, and has several other characteristics still present in the design of modern boards.

No matter what their design, the boards of the earliest period were dried in the sun after use, coated with coconut oil, and then hung on the wall of their owners' dwellings. The more meticulous owners sheathed them in cloth to give the wood further protection.

Rocked by the Waves

The practice of he'e nalu transcended the dimension of sport and the realm of simple pastime. It was really integrated into the way of life of the early Hawaiians. Although it may not have been a practice with a specifically religious connotation, certain rituals were connected with it, particularly at the time of making the board and on the occasion of its first use. The hope of seeing beautiful waves prompted various cultural manifestations, including the following ancient chant, offered on the occasion of an annual celebration of surfing in 1896 and passed on to us by Gault-Williams:

> In'a'ohe nalu, a laila aku i kai, penei e hea ai:
> Kumai! Kumai! Ka nalu nui mai Kahiki mai,
> Alo po'i pu! Ku mai ka pohuehue,
> Hu! Kai ko'o loa.

> If there is no surf, invoke seaward in the following manner:
> Arise! Arise, you great surfs from Kahiki,
> The powerful curling waves,
> Well up, long raging surf.[5]

And when the waves so long awaited and so ardently yearned for began to roll in, the Hawaiians dropped all other occupations in order to surf. Spurred on by a passion for the pleasures of life, the Hawaiians, like all Polynesians, gave surfing, but also dancing, a place of priority in organizing the activities of their everyday life. The festivals during which surfing and dancing took place were ongoing and provided the occasion for other manifestations of Polynesian culture, such as chanting, playing music, and gambling. They also permitted the sexes to interact in a completely free fashion. If a woman and a man found themselves surfing the same wave at the same time, this was sometimes interpreted as a coincidence signifying that the two of them were meant for each other. The tradition of people coupling up spontaneously without an elaborate courtship and without stated commitments to live together may have evolved with the parallel tradition of children being raised by the entire community. It may be difficult for us to understand this very different lifestyle in which there is no word meaning "orphan" in the original Hawaiian language.[6]

Through the work of Rell Sun, a Hawaiian who devoted a good part of her life to conducting and organizing celebrations connected with surfing for young Hawaiians,[7] the love that Hawaiians feel for young people is evident. Here we see an interesting cultural model that aims at integrating future generations into the present one in an atmosphere that promotes a sense of freedom while instilling confidence and respect.

Beyond the historical details and names of ancestral heroes—the legends and tales having to do with the deeds of Polynesian royalty are numerous—what is important to keep in mind is that the navigation of the blue territory of the planet was first of all an adventure in the Eastern hemisphere, driven by necessity and a curiosity to learn of the spaces the earth had to offer. The result of this was a culture made unique among humanity by the priority it placed on the pleasure and spontaneity that arise from an intense relationship with nature, with others, and with oneself.

The Visions of the West

In December 1777 the famous sea captain and explorer James Cook landed on Tahiti, at Matavi Point to be precise, and saw a surfer using a canoe in the fashion of a surfboard. Cook perceived the activity as an amusement that possessed, it seemed, the virtue of being able to dissipate the troubles of the mind as successfully as music. Here is how he described the final moments of the scene he witnessed:

> He then sat motionless, and was carried along at the same swift rate as the wave, till it landed him upon the beach. Then he started out . . . and went in search of another swell. I could not help concluding that this man felt the most supreme pleasure while he was driven on so fast and so smoothly by the sea.[8]

The writer and traveler Isabella Bird, at the beginning of the nineteenth century, presented surfing as a noble activity, while other observers, particularly the missionary Hiram Bingham (who landed in Hawaii in 1820), depicted it in much less glowing terms. In the history of surfing as it has been written, we find a duality expressed in the commentaries of the authors, who qualified the activity on the one hand as "the most exciting pastime" and "a great art" and on the other hand as "destitution, degradation and bar-barism."

Cook arrived in Waimea, Kauai in Hawaii in 1778, and about two years later the first missionaries arrived on the island and discovered, to their outrage, the practice that Cook had been able to appreciate. Surfing and the customs that surrounded it obviously shocked the soldiers of God, and they did not fail to note that this activity, because of the amount of time the Hawaiians devoted to it, limited the potential for profits that could be developed from the exploitation of this new world. We can see today that although these religious men were working for the salvation of humanity, they also gave priority in their minds to the progress and development of the West:

> Surfing was against the hand of God, said the missionaries, although it was not to the surfing specifically that they objected, but to the associated sins, "the betting, the sexual freedom, and men and women surfing together in scanty costumes." Time was being wasted which could be better used for learning and hard manual work."[9]

In the early 1800s, Queen Kaahumanu, the wife of King Kamehameha I, who was impressed by, among other things, the white people's ability to tell stories and their use of a written language, converted to their religion. She became a good friend of Hiram Bingham, an influential missionary. Although King Kamehameha—an imposing personage more than two meters (six and a half feet) tall—had peacefully welcomed the first Europeans to arrive in his territory, he quickly became aware of their greed. Several wars followed in which many Europeans perished, including Cook himself in 1779. Kamehameha finally returned to peaceful terms with the foreigners around 1812 and eventually came to accept their presence. The Russians landed in 1816, and soon many other immigrants followed, profiting from a period of economic growth that began to affect the island at this time. The largest immigrant groups were the Japanese, the Filipinos, and the Chinese, ethnic groups that still figure prominently in the Hawaiian community.

In the heart of the queen, as her friendship with Bingham grew stronger, the traditional Hawaiian values dwindled away, gradually replaced by European Calvinism. One fine day, Kaahumanu commanded that the temples be destroyed, along with other objects that were thought to contribute to the perpetuation of the ancient values. From that point on, the Hawaiians found their favorite activities were branded with a negative connotation, including surfing, partying, singing, dancing, playing music, going naked, gambling, drinking, and freely making love. The repression of these practices limited the transmission of a tradition that had perpetuated itself chiefly through these activities, as well as through stories and traditional chants. The feasts and festivals connected with surfing came to an end, and the Hawaiians, given the social context of the period, had little choice but to accept the authority of their venerable queen, authority that was further invoked by her physical grace and poise and the fact that she stood nearly two meters (more than six feet) tall.

The Hawaiians, having managed to survive the diseases brought by the Europeans now died literally and figuratively owing to the loss of what had inspired and animated them and had assured the survival of their unique lifestyle. From the 200,000 they had numbered at the time of Cook's arrival, they were reduced to 132,315 at the time of the first census in 1832, and in 1878 there were no more than 50,000 Hawaiians left.[10] In the last quarter of the nineteenth century, there was a small revival of the spirit of he'e nalu, thanks to the young king Kamehameha III. Then came King Kalakaua, who worked to rehabilitate the chants and other cultural elements by organizing festivals at Waikiki, but he did not have a successor. Thus, on the cusp of the twentieth century, it could be said that almost all that was left of the practice of surfing were the artifacts preserved in the museums.

In 1895 there remained just a few indomitable traditional surfers at Waikiki, the center of the surviving indigenous population. Surfing could still be seen there, but the techniques had regressed. Surfers rode the waves in a crouched position—a fetal position, with the back curved and bent. The boards had reverted to a crude form, because most of those who had mastered the art of authentic papa he'e nalu were dead and buried. Surfing as a culture had almost disappeared; only rarely were there spectators. Among the diehards at Waikiki, there was a woman by the name of Kaiulaini who contributed a certain feminine atmosphere to the surfing of the period. She rode an olo made of wili wili, one of the rare boards that bridged the gap between the former generations and the modern ones to come.

A New Wave

There is no official date that marks the revival of surfing, but 1898 is often mentioned. That was the year in which Thomas Edison, the inventor of the phonograph and the electric lightbulb, first immortalized surfing on film.

Starting in 1903, the small circles of surfing were infused with new life by a certain Duke Paoa Kahino Mokoe Hukilikohala Kahanamoku, to this day a legendary character in Hawaii, where an enormous statue has been erected in his honor. He has also been honored in the same fashion in Australia. Recognized as the father of modern surfing, the Duke, as he was called, began around this time (he was about fifteen years old) to become passionately involved in informal meetings with his friends at which they discussed their surfing experiences. From these meetings, the Waikiki Swimming Club developed. Having first learned to swim in rather dramatic fashion—his father had simply thrown him from his canoe off the shore of Waikiki when he was eleven years old—Duke Kahanamoku, who benefited from an athletic physique, was a great swimmer. At forty-two years old, he was still an active member of the American Olympic water polo team, able to swim the hundred meters in 59.8 seconds.

A few years later, in 1907, George Freeth, a veteran swimmer and a good surfer, is thought to have revived the practice of standing completely erect on the surfboard. What was particularly noteworthy about Freeth was that he was a "white man," and there was a long-standing belief that "white men" couldn't surf. Through his dedication to the promotion of surfing, Freeth to some extent redeemed the intolerance of his European ancestors. He was incredibly dynamic and was instrumental in revitalizing the practice of surfing at Waikiki. He popularized a technique of surfing that consists of moving diagonally across the waves, making it possible to use their force more efficiently. He also helped to popularize surfing in California, where it had first been introduced in Santa Cruz in 1885 by Hawaiian students. The eminent writer Jack London was one of Freeth's disciples and became an important and much-needed spokesman for Hawaiian surfing during this time of its renaissance. London was introduced to Freeth by Alexander Hume Ford, founder in 1907 of the Outrigger Canoe Club, the first official organization whose mission was to preserve the heritage of surfing.

Surfing was established once and for all on the American continent during this period, when Freeth was employed by the Pacific Electric Railroad, which was trying to extend its service to include Redondo Beach. The railroad company saw in Freeth's surfing a good means for promoting the service it was offering to the beach and began advertising nothing less than the spectacle of "a man able to walk on water." The fact that Freeth's travels had been described in the writings of Jack London was surely of no little help in the success of this marketing operation. In this way George Freeth became the first professional surfer, as well as the first official lifeguard on the Pacific Coast. He later devoted himself to training champion swimmers. Freeth's rescues of drowning persons from the waves made the headlines more than once, and his name became synonymous with bravery. After having received many accolades and a number of awards for his courage, a village near Port Angeles was renamed for him, and Freeth became a national hero. He died prematurely in 1912 at the age of thirty-five, at the end of a career as a lifeguard in which he had saved the lives of seventy-eight people. On account of the reputation he earned through his professional activities and his personal dedication, George Freeth can be seen as the man who planted the seed of the Californian culture of surfing in America.

The Final Impetus

At the beginning of the twentieth century, tourism began to flourish in Hawaii. The construction of large hotels made it increasingly evident to Hawaiians that the beach was becoming the territory of foreigners. The revival of surfing became a way of cultivating Hawaiians's awareness of their heritage and its relationship to the sea. Within this context, the Hawaiians discovered that the values connected with the practice of aquatic sports, which had been denigrated by the missionaries, were now held in high esteem by other Europeans. This shift in status was an important factor in the unconditional dedication of people like the Duke, Freeth, Ford, and others of this period. Once again history will show that it takes many individuals whose actions are underpinned by their energetic convictions to have the power to change things in this world.

The Duke won a gold medal swimming the one hundred meters at the 1912 Olympic Games in Sweden. He did it again in 1920 at the Games at Antwerp, where, in addition, he shared gold medals in the sports of water polo and relay swimming. After these victories, he made a series of trips to promote surfing—in Australia among other places—and continued the work of popularizing surfing in California. He was an international ambassador of surfing. From 1920 to 1925 he was an actor in Hollywood, after which time he returned to Hawaii and took on the title of sheriff, a position that was more honorary than lucrative. In 1961, his name was commercialized by Kimo Wilder McVay, who used it to market a line of surfing products. He died in 1968 at the age of seventy-seven of a heart attack.

In 1924 Tom Blake, an acquaintance of the Duke's and an equally good swimmer, arrived in Hawaii to practice surfing, which he had discovered in California in 1921. He contributed to the development of surfing by inventing the fin, which makes it possible to control the direction of the board better and thereby also to reach higher speeds. Two years later, it was Lauren Thurston who came up with a further innovation. He introduced a new wood, lighter than any that had been used before, balsa. During this period of technical development, there was also a lot of prospecting for surfing spots, and Blake, who split his surfing time between Hawaii and California, made the historic discovery, along with his friend Sam Reid, of the mystical beach of Malibu. It was a private beach at the time it was first surfed by Blake and Reid, but it became public a few years later and the favorite meeting place for the in-crowd adepts of a growing counterculture.

Tom Blake tirelessly pursued his research toward improving equipment, and in 1929, inspired by an old Hawaiian design, he created the "cigar board," a board that performed so well that the following year it was used officially in the races of the Annual Surfboard Paddling Championship in Hawaii. The event was dominated by none other than Blake himself. All at once his board became popular among lifeguard teams throughout America. Blake, in 1935, was also the first to publish a book on the art of surfing: *Hawaiian Surfboard*. In this recently reprinted work (as *Hawaiian Surfboard, 1935*), Tom Blake described surfing as "a sport of peace and prosperity."[11]

In 1939 the Second World War broke out and the surfing culture left Hawaii—now too strategically important to remain a holiday spot—and continued its evolution in California. During this period the freedom to surf was limited, but discoveries that derived from military research introduced surfboard designers to new materials. In 1946 Peter Peterson, who with Lorrin Harrison was one of the best surfers of the prewar period, introduced the first board made of nylon and fiberglass. Bob Simmons put together fiberglass and balsa wood, contributed to the development of the science of surfing by taking an interest in weather maps, and began making popular the American lifestyle associated with surfing by sleeping in his car with his board, waiting for the best waves. Traveling up and down the California coast full-time, Simmons disappeared during a surfing session in 1954.

The Beat of the Ride

The period of the 1950s and 1960s was marked on the technical level by new applications of the nylon and fiberglass that had been introduced in the late 1940s. Starting at this point, we can speak of the first real modern performance levels. Finally surfers were able to climb back up a wave and pivot on its lip. Surfing style became more acrobatic and began to foreshadow the period of aerial maneuvers that was to come.

On the societal level, this was the period when images of surfing began to pervade the media. The year 1960 marked the founding of *Surfer Magazine* by John Severson. The following year, the rival magazine *Surfing* hit the stands. In 1964 the first world championship of surfing was organized, and an Australian, Midget Farrelly, took the prize. That same year the film *Endless Summer* came out, directed by Bruce Brown. The plot is simple but effective: two surfers travel the world, wandering in nature and discovering waves of unimaginable beauty. The film, after a tentative start, became a worldwide success. The surfing lifestyle became the ideal of many young American men, while their "surf widows" awaited them on the sands.

As more and more beach vagabonds came to wander the California coast, a growing gap developed between the reality of a youthful generation in quest of freedom and the imagination of a media-conditioned public. Surfing culture was depicted as a fundamentally antiestablishment way of life, and the idea of surfers as social deviants began to spread.

The image of the surfer in the literature of the nineteenth century drew on the myth of the mysterious noble savage. At the beginning of the 1960s, it evolved into depicting surfers as dangerous to society. From that point on, the surfer became a punk in the public eye, an immoral, rebellious, and anticonformist element. According to journalist Matt Warshaw, surfers reacted to this set of prejudices by joining together as a common front to break certain social conventions. This all happened around 1965, the era that produced Beatlemania, Bob Dylan's "Talkin' John Birch Society Blues," and the Berkeley free-speech movement.

For American advocates of the puritan way of life, surfing at this moment symbolized nothing less than the end of civil society. During this time the surfing media (*Surfer*, 1963) expressed concerns that the image of surfing was being degraded by the dilettantes, and gremmies, and the music associated with surf riding. A confrontation was clearly taking place, and society demanded of surfers that they define their universe in a socially acceptable fashion, compatible with established values.

It was *Gidget*, the book published by Frederick Kohner in 1957, that provided an occasion for the general public to rediscover the romantic dimension of surfing. In this story the heart of the heroine is divided between two youths, one a model student and another a vagabond of the beaches. Warshaw highlights the moment of insight found at the conclusion of the work when Gidget (the main character) reflects on the love she felt for these two young men and compares it to her love of surfing: "But with the board and the sun and the waves, it was for real. All things considered—maybe I was just a woman in love with a surfboard. It's as simple as that."[12]

The revolutionary attitude associated with surfing also reached Europe. The years from 1950 to 1970 are the first two decades of the major spread of the spirit of surfing, and when surfing crossed the Atlantic (to France in 1956), an international community of surfers was formed and consolidated. The good Californian surfers returned en masse to Hawaii after the war and reconnected there with the original spirit of surfing. Pat Curren, George Dowing, Peter Cole, and Greg Noll, through their exploits on the big waves, particularly at Waimea, revived the desire to create boards that would make it possible to open new frontiers.

The Return to the East

In the seventies, thanks to films like *Endless Summer* and the quest for the perfect wave it depicted, surfing became explicitly associated with nomadism and the spirit of adventure that had characterized surfing's ancestors. Competitions were established throughout the world, contributing to the internationalization of the movement as well as to the idea of spontaneous travel associated with it. In 1976 the first professional tour was created—once again it was Australia that provided the champion, a surfer by the name of Peter Townend.

On the technical front, boards became shorter and more stream-lined. Performance continued to become more refined, and with the help of ever lighter materials, surfers began to explore maneuvers in the air. Sideslides on the lip of the wave, followed by jumps—moves that came out of California—marked this period. It was also during the seventies that the double fin, which allows greater speed with better balance, came into use and spread.

This new period of surfing was also one in which surfers began to explore the experience of the tube ever further. People like Gerry Lopez—a surfer who was also an accomplished yoga practitioner and who made a significant contribution to the development of surf-ing during the seventies—pushed back the frontiers. Everywhere in the world, young people were hitting the road to surf. Yves Bessas, a French surfer and writer who popularized the term *glisse*, meaning "riding" or "free riding," conveys the spirit of the times quite well in his tale of a voyage of initiation lasting two years, during which he surfed the most beautiful waves in the world. Bessas's journey took him to South America, California, New Zealand, and Hawaii, among other places. In Hawaii he visited the Pipeline and there he had the opportunity to observe Lopez at work at the height of his powers:

> Gerry Lopez . . . slithered like an eel down the walls of the tubes. There was never a superfluous movement, super-relaxed, with his arms dangling in the face of this menacing wall, he was at play. The perfection of his moves shows composure and concentration far beyond the ordinary.[13]

In the course of his journey, Bessas discovered a Californian philosophy of surfing that enabled him, along with an array of new disciplines that he integrated into his lifestyle—meditation, yoga, and Chinese medicine—to attain a certain inner peace, to "regulate the flow of his energy, [to live] in a state of harmony with the elements, in contemplation."[14] Rejecting a life in which everything seemed to be imposed on him, in an environment in which people seemed to him like prisoners, Yves Bessas bore witness in his book, *La Glisse*, to a new way of looking at the world, the outlook of a surfer "who feels himself becoming a man of nature."[15] His view of society became very critical, and on his return from a trip to South America, he had a vision of civilization, of the modern way of life that he had left behind:

My arrival in Texas was dramatic. This change in lifestyle is too radical, especially as far as food is concerned. Everything is wrapped in plastic, frozen, or refrigerated. The cities are like huge air-conditioned hospitals. Everything alive seems to have withdrawn from them. We have the impression of passing through regions that have been devastated by a cataclysm. We are taking in nothing but negative vibrations. It is as though a plague were gnawing at the brain, at the thoughts, at the life of people.[16]

The rest of the book is often more cheerful, and the author, who in my opinion gives a very intense account of the world of the ride, moves from one description to the next, each one more stimulating than the last. Transformed by his new lifestyle, he tells a story that,

for me, revives that zest for life we all share. His journey gave him a
new, inspired viewpoint:

> I feel myself being carried along. An incredible area of
> wave is above and over me. I am enclosed in a tunnel of
> transparent water with the opening ten meters in front
> of me. I'm scared, but at the same time an unspeakable
> pleasure rises up my spine. . . . In fetal position, I hang
> close to the wall of the tube, my eyes wide open, my
> mouth agape. The notion of time disappears. As in astral
> travel, my body is at one with my will to be projected into
> the light. No more fear, only a violent orgasmic feeling
> that is tremendously powerful and gentle at the same
> time.[17]

The Californian way of life lived by Bessas, and described by
Jean-Pierre Augustin in a collection devoted entirely to this theme,
pushed back the frontiers of the West toward the East. Here was a
search for new approaches, a will to see what is good in the combination of these two poles of the human horizon:

> It [California] gave birth to the Beatnik movement and the
> Hippie movement, to the movement of the revival of sects
> and religious feelings that consecrated new gurus, and
> also gave birth to the cult of the body. The priests of the
> New Age promulgated a specific spirituality: the body is a
> temple for the mind—whatever you do for it will nourish
> the soul."[18]

In this sense, devoting oneself to surfing was fortifying one's temple, giving oxygen to the soul, nourishing the link between mind and matter. In short, this was a culture of an existence of intense vibrations in which human beings find themselves at the core of self as well as at the center of the elements that compose the environment.

The 1980s: The Fun Years

Design continued to progress during the 1980s, when boards became shorter, generally less than two meters (six and a half feet) long. Also during this period, the triple fin was introduced. Following this development, surfing gave birth to a new set of riding devices. Many of these had already been in the works for some time, but it was not until the beginning of the 1980s that they took definite hold. We are speaking of snowboards and skateboards, as well as many other vehicles to ride, which at that time began to appear on a massive scale. At this time also, the use of the longboard made a comeback, after a bit of a lag following the high-performance shorter boards. This was the beginning of the "If it feels good, do it" era.

An interesting phenomenon is the way the culture of surfing, in addition to being idealized by the general public and associated with the quest for freedom, also influenced many other sports, where the sensation of the ride, in which the limits of the human being as a whole are explored, could be discovered and cultivated. This happened when the practitioners of those sports were willing to let go of the conventions and rules of competition and began to move and ride for the fun of it. They sought the act, the movement itself, rather than victory and status. They took part in sporting events first and foremost just to participate. This was a refreshing attitude that was cleverly picked up by the sports-shoe maker Nike, who filled the advertising spaces of the period with their dynamic "Just do it" campaign.

Starting at this moment, the concept of the ride began to lose a part of its meaning and context. The advertising people tried to extend the world of surfing beyond the waves. More and more they injected notions like "surfing is fun" into advertising copy directed at the general public. "Fun" became the sought-after sensation of more and more people.

This democratization of "fun" was followed by the popularization of "surfwear" and then "streetwear." This was fashion with an alternative character that has become so common that we often forget that it derives from a lifestyle connected with surfing. The traditional colors used for athletic wear gave way to a wave of fluorescents that flooded the ready-to-wear athletic clothing market. This recharging of the market arose out of the psychedelic movement led by Timothy Leary, among others, a writer who in California at the beginning of the 1960s preached individual creativity and expansion of consciousness by way of the ingestion of lysergic acid (LSD). Its development clearly shows how the movement of dissent against the "American way of life" had spread, passing beyond small artistic circles to the point where, in twenty years, it had reached the level of mass socialization on the largest scale via the intermediary of popular sports.

The rediscovery of pop art and beat literature, which sang the praises of life "on the road," as well as a variety of other movements, such as ska—originally a Jamaican, then a British movement that advocated a nonviolent revolution with ethnic tolerance as the goal—energized creative artists, magazine editors, and advertising people who developed copy related to riding. The exploration of these countercultural ideas from earlier decades became a prevailing source of inspiration, and dissent was no longer just the affair of a few beach bums, hippies, or freaks à la Frank Zappa. Rather, it became the new content of cool and was on the tongues of all the young people.

Scanning the Future

> Maybe surfers will be the ones to show the world how to take care of our planet and how to enjoy it without borders.
> —Reinaldo Andraus, Brazilian surfer

Human beings do not travel in time, they travel in humanity. Time, on the scale of the cosmos, is unimaginable. The world has tried at the onset of a new century to find a reference point, proof that something has progressed, advanced. Our minds are now so agitated because of conflicts linked to the push to get the cultures of the world globalized, repressions of diversity, and the condition of waiting for a significant event to occur, it's as though being were incapable of setting anything in motion on its own. Nonetheless, currents of thought advocating freedom based on respect for diversity, as well as the idea that each person has power over reality and first of all over him- or herself, keep coming back to the surface. Self-help books are bringing in big money. New heroes, driven by the concept of freedom, are striving to discover what's out there—beyond the biggest wave, in the depths of the earth, at the limits of outer space, or within being itself. They feel compelled to always climb higher, in the hope of attaining a larger view. It's already obvious in the natural world, but difficult for *Homo sapiens* to accept, that our place in it is so terribly small and insignificant. In the microcosm of surfing, this quest for truth in extremes has now taken the form of competition in which the winner is the person who catches the biggest wave or expresses their grand ideas by inventing new practices, such as towing. This practice of modern surfing consists in a surfer being towed by a motorized craft in order to take on waves that are too fast and too big to be caught by using human strength alone, waves that are sometimes as high as fifteen meters (fifty feet). While those who do this seem to derive immense pleasure from it, old-school surfers are a bit disturbed by it all and are wondering what it could be leading to:

> I don't understand it, really. I mean, they're out there in a
> different world. Gettin' towed in . . . they're haulin' ass, I
> know that. Heavy, fifteen inch wide boards! It's a little
> hard to relate to, but I'm all for 'em. Eventually,
> something is going to come out of it—I don't know what
> they're doing. I'm not sure they know yet. But it's
> definitely a new direction.[19]

While some businesses are mass-producing boards designed to fall apart within a predetermined period of time, others are returning to older, more utopian approaches—a case in point being unbreakable boards. The Californian company Patagonia brought this idea back in 1997 when it entered the surfing industry and introduced strong, epoxy-type resins derived from natural sources. The same ideas continue to spin around and around. More proof of this came in 1994, when the film *Endless Summer II* appeared. Bruce Brown, three decades after putting out *Endless Summer*, reused his old formula for success, changing the plot very little and once again giving the place of honor in the movie to the most beautiful things nature has to offer.

Thanks in part to the films, but especially moved by their desire to have "fun," more and more people are riding. This has led Nelson Paillon, the president of the French National Olympic and Sports Committee, to reflect: "We must succeed in officially including sports of the new type, such as surfing, paragliding, parachuting, and the triathlon. These are disciplines that correspond to the tastes of the people of today. We must preserve the tradition of Olympic sports, but evolve, because the taste of people evolves."[20] Sports transform attitudes, which in turn transform sports, and one fine day, our minds will have to readapt. Are we dealing with historical cycles here, or are these really new realities?

While some of us search for the absolute and others try to catch up with the flavor-of-the-moment, most surfers remain content just to watch the waves so they can catch them at their peak, happy to have contact with nature in a way that turns them on. From the first moments of gliding on the waves, despite a plethora of improvements in design and technique, what is essential has no more changed than time itself:

Surfing exists in its own time. It is its own time. There is no real anachronism, and no postsynchronization either: here everything is immediately simultaneous, synchronized. There is no history, in actual fact, even though the old surfers recount the history of the long-gone longboards of smoothed wood. Surfing has no past and no future, it just waits, entirely in the present moment, for the next wave. Which actually will come, and many more as well. They are already virtually formed, just in a different present.[21]

3 | Planet Surf

We have by now gone far beyond the idea that surfing is only a game, a diversion for disillusioned teenagers ready to do anything for a thrill, who know no fear because they value their lives so little. More than a matter of powerful sensations, surfing is a quest for balance and self-control. Not only do the surfers love life, but they see it through constantly refreshed senses, ever and again stimulated by a contact with nature that makes them conceive of their existence in personal terms. The surfer has ideals and a unique way of organizing his or her life, at least when near the sea. Moving in the midst of the elements, a surfer learns to see the world differently than the modern urbanite, who has been sickened by stress and pushed by the mind-set of production toward a representation of the world in which everything must be evaluated, accounted for, and paid for. On the sea, on a board, one makes one's effort for free, and the reward has no price tag.

My goal here is of course to inform, but it is also to entertain the reader and to encourage you to take a mental journey into the world of surfing that exists now. I would like you to imagine how, with just a board and a mad desire to surf, it is possible to penetrate a parallel universe. I would like to show that passion, with a force multiplied tenfold by will and action, can create worlds that go beyond dreams and illusions.

Seeking balance by means of riding free means accepting a loss of control. It means exploring a world that is sometimes bewildering in its dynamism and constant change. Riding, by definition, is a state of transition. It is ephemeral motion.

Moreover, when we speak of the culture of surfing, we can't forget that what is involved is a combination of elements always evolving in various directions. There are as many visions of surfing as there are practitioners busy advancing them. The individuality and plurality of the experience of riding make certain that on the cultural level, change will be perpetual. Surfing evolves over time and under the influence of the people who cultivate its spirit.

Planet Surf is a world shared between the industrialized sport, in which performance and competition provide numbers to be calculated, and an entirely different reality—one in which the essential thing is to swim, to laugh, and just to surf because the wave is there, here and now; and because the surfer is well and truly alive, at the center of himself, having abandoned himself to the explosive joys brought on by the simple fact of being there.

Respect and Hope (the Storm)

> Besides 20- to 35-foot waves, nothing scares me. I fear no man. And I'm not so much afraid of huge waves; it's just a matter of respect for the ocean.
>
> —John Gomes, surfer

For some, surfing the waves is an aquatic sport; for others, it is riding in an upside-down world, natural, eternal, and ultimately indefinable, a world in which the individual is sometimes insignificant, fused with the horizon, and in which fear of the fall, of the last and fateful tumble, is often present.

In this environment, transforming fear and anxiety into respect seems to be the secret. At least, that is the opinion of those who view the planet from that special perspective high on the crests of the waves.

For many business people, surfers are marginal creatures, who have forsaken a financial future to pursue the life of a drifter, or even a bum. To their peers, they are at the very least other individuals who are searching, separating themselves from the distractions of artifice and its epileptic machines for making money; someone who is looking for the energy of life, advancing by the power of the light. The light of the sun, of which the wave, the point of meeting and the point where riding can happen, is the third eye. It looks at every-thing from a point of view of total impunity.

Coming out of the waves, the surfer "comes back from another world,"[22] a world where what is dramatic and dangerous for some people is instead a source of exaltation. "Nothing excites a good Australian surfer more than a cyclone forming off the coast of Queensland."[23] Many surfers maintain a special relationship with nature and its magnetic manifestations, such as storms, tornadoes, and other frolics of the wind.

Surfers have their own ideas about the relationship between human beings and the elements—with attitudes ranging from the greatest respect to an ambition for conquest. They are often very well informed about the storm cycles and other factors that govern the waves. They are tuned in. This is an essential cultural vestige of the original Polynesian heritage. Some, like Sean Collins, an extraordinary surf rider, have even made this into a path, a way of communicating and of conferring a meaning to their being. Their challenge is to determine, through their skill and intuition, where and when the next storm will strike and what manner of waves it will produce. In the case of Collins, his intuitions are good, and reputable meteorologists and oceanographers acknowledge his talent: "Collins is the guru. He was the first to add it all up."[24] In the quest for the perfect wave or in the search for the hugest monument made of water, a surfer like Collins counts for a lot. In another, more mythical, context, he would be called a shaman, a seer, or a chief.

Today technology stands in the stead of magic. The data that wave farers accumulate is now made available via telephone lines, and a business has been promoted by Sunny Garcia—a surfer of high repute—that electronically transmits surfing conditions to its subscribers. For surfers this is the best of worlds, where everything is done to avoid the waste of good waves, a resource impossible to replace.

In point of fact, the fury of the ocean cannot be reproduced in a swimming pool, and everyone is agreed, when riding a wave that lasts and lasts, that it is a gift, a gift made entirely out of water. No matter how much money a person may have, no one can buy the sensations that come through surfing. You have to be there when the wave rolls, present with all your being, ready to paddle in order to savor an event that can never be repeated in the same way again.

The Waves, to Be Exact

Rolling and swaying, waves are served up as fruit, the fruit of waiting. Waves define a universe made of round curves the color of glass. Rare is the person who does not enjoy contemplating their rhythmic beauty. Some people are unable to resist plunging into them, while others remain seated on the beach, meditatively appreciating the sounds. The sound of wind in the leaves of trees, the batting of eyelashes, sighs of the heart, sand in an hourglass—many phenomena of ordinary life recall the cycle and essence of the waves, evoking their ephemeral quality, just as does the shooting star that disappears. We must admit that the particular character of the waveform in general—which gives birth to sea waves and builds the image of the world (is it really no more than a collection of vibrations between orbiting atoms?)—expresses a profound resonance of truth, an audible rumble, a song of nature announcing that life has come onto the scene.

So, waves. Let us have a quick look at how they develop and are unleashed. First, it is really the wind, itself created by the sun warming masses of air above the earth, that is the origin of the whole phenomenon. The wind blows on the surface of the sea, which starts out as smooth as molasses; then nearly invisible undulations form and circulate in all directions on our planet. Under the influence of these undulations, cones of energy form, evolving like spirals around an axis, and they rise from the sea bottom upward, then return back from the top toward the abyss.

The wave travels and travels, the wind blows and blows. The energy of the cone increases, and the undulations take on amplitude.

They develop height and continue their voyage in groups of four. This grouping of four undulations, in which each one travels faster than the group as a result of a phenomenon of circular succession, constitutes a potential wave that will take form in accordance with the morphology of the coast where its journey will end. An abrupt falling away of the bottom, a long, gentle slope, or an abrupt and deep one—these are the variables that give the wave beginning to tumble upon itself an unsurfable quality or a lofty face worthy of the masters.

The tide also affects the curves and lips of the waves by exposing the sea bottom to varying degrees, but it never causes a single wave all by itself. As to the final form of the wave, this again is a product of the wind's talent. When it blows seaward from the land, it smoothes the faces of the waves, evens out the imperfections, and causes the roundest of tubes to reach their ultimate apotheosis.

As for the great tsunamis, devastating tidal waves, these are seismic in origin, caused by undersea avalanches or movements of tectonic plates. A tsunami travels very discreetly, without the help of the wind, so discreetly you cannot see it coming. When the sea draws back fast from the shore, when animals begin to run in all directions because something invisible is stimulating their senses, then you can begin to suspect one is coming. But by then it is often too late. That is why in Japan, Indonesia, and many other places in the Pacific, people and entire villages and towns, such as in Anchorage, Alaska, in 1964 and more recently, in Papua New Guinea in July 1998, are sometimes swallowed up by these monster waves. A Godzilla made of water, the tsunami can attain a height of thirty-five meters (115 feet) after having traveled an enormous distance at an average speed of 725 kilometers (450 miles) per hour, as was the case in 1883, at the time of the eruption of the Indonesian volcano, Krakatau (formerly Krakatoa). Around thirty-six thousand dead were counted on the coasts of the various oceans of the globe traveled by the tsunami. Thirteen years later, in 1896, a wave of even greater immensity struck Honshu, Japan, killing almost twenty-seven thousand human beings. This is not a phenomenon that involves only the Pacific Ocean, if we are to believe this note in the Montreal daily newspaper *Le Devoir* of March 12, 1998.

> One of Environment Canada's buoys last October measured a wave of record height 250 kilometers southwest of Nova Scotia. This wave, with no known precedents, was more than thirty meters in height, which is the equivalent of a ten-story building. It is possible that the wave in question was even higher than that. The measuring apparatus, although it did not malfunction, had gone beyond its measuring limit. No wave of this size has ever been measured by instruments before. We can appreciate the importance of the preparations that are undertaken on the basis of these buoy measurements on the high seas when we consider that the most modern of North American oil-drilling platforms, the Hibernia, is built to resist a wave of thirty-five meters.

Such waves are not for surfing, but they still inspire all surfers, both the wee ones and the adults, filling them with hope, which stands in opposition to the fear that buffets the titans of the world of black gold as they worry over their oil-drilling platforms. For the surfer, these immense waves represent an essential, almost unimaginable ideal; they are a symbol of the boundless immensity of nature. Everything, it seems, is a matter of perception.

And what is the role of El Niño in all this? As to the basic facts, El Niño corresponds to an abnormal elevation in the temperature of the equatorial waters of the Pacific. This warming of oceanic waters causes a warming of the atmosphere by means of heat transfer (there is a major exchange of gases where the ocean and atmosphere meet). Since the water mass of the Pacific communicates with those of the other oceans, the climate is quickly influenced on a global scale.

The exact cause of El Niño has not been determined, but global warming, amplified by the polluting activities of a certain biped animal who is supposedly endowed with reason and imagination, *Homo modernus*, is strongly suspected. The reactions of this animal are varied. For example, if he or she is a surfer, this cataclysm is something that warms the surfer's heart. This is not because surfers are indifferent to the environment but rather because storms provoked by El Niño produce waves like never before: "Surfers in search of the perfect ride are enjoying the thrills of a lifetime thanks to El Niño."[25] From photographs of the effect to fictitious interviews with El Niño by telephone, surfing magazines have covered the phenomenon from the moment it was identified and interpreted by weather specialists. In some ways it is like a minor deity, a little angry spirit, and the surfers—instead of apologizing for their celebrations or fearing this force whose message is that civilized beings need to stop polluting—are doing a dance to keep it alive and lend it further vigor. It is their idea to draw attention to a playful dimension within this hint of apocalypse, this consequence of the bad treatment we have given Mother Nature.

4 | Sirens and Other Metaphors of Nature

According to Greek mythology, the sea is inhabited by mysterious women, the Nereids. Represented by the waves, they are said to be of great beauty, living in harmony with the dolphins, bathing their long hair in the sea, singing, and weaving embroidery from the sea foam.

The Nereid is in fact a siren, a well-known symbol. I say "symbol" because the siren seems to be a product of the human imagination. On the other hand, reality often goes beyond fiction. The siren does indeed sometimes appear in the fantastic world of the surf. We experience her palpable curves and her changeable energy. Surfers are inspired by or fantasize about her image and the idea she expresses. The siren's image can be seen painted on surfboards here and there, or from time to time in a mural at the back of a restaurant or bar frequented by aficionados of the ride.

What the siren represents for surfers evokes several elements of their environment. It is a broader concept than the mere image of an idealized feminine body. In the context of surfing, the siren's qualities evoke a sense of liberation that can be calming, even orgasmic in nature; but she brings suffering as well, for "she always delivers horror along with ecstasy,"[26] in the same way as the mega-wave, which brings surfers intense pleasure and at the same time the possibility of death.[27]

There is no doubt that the sea has a feminine symbolic value. Titles of surfing songs like "Mama Nature" or the title of the most recent album put out to benefit the Surfrider Foundation, *For Our Mother Ocean*, and a host of other examples abundantly illustrate the conceptual link that exists between femininity, the mysteries of life, and natural forces. Of course this association is found in many other contexts aside from surfing:

> Her power to give Life and provide Nourishment encourages us to believe, as many myths attest, that woman has intimate links with the cosmic forces. This makes of her a magician par excellence. And the phantasmagoric, mythical power attributed to woman goes even further than that, if we are to believe the revelations of psychoanalysis.[28]

Becoming One with Nature

The surfer, who is of a "race that is still capable of touching, tasting, feeling, and hearing . . . in order to perceive the world,"[29] intuitively seeks to deepen their relationship with the cosmos, attempting to go beyond the human condition as it is conceived of by modern society. From this perspective, becoming one with the sea or a siren does not appear to be such an extravagant notion:

> Surfing, riding a wave, is a dream. . . . But it is a dream come true. Over the time the wave lasts, the surfer evolves in a multicolored "somewhere else" that is almost unreal, sometimes perfect. The unimaginable exists in life. Surfing is a surrealistic sport.[30]

Since surfers, while riding, go beyond human existence as it is "realistically" conceived, it is easy to see how, in the rest of their life, they would seek to break through all frontiers, or at least to try what other people consider to be unrealistic.

Transcending human nature, linking oneself with an existence of a higher intensity, penetrating to the heart of a universal consciousness—these are surely motivations that are born from contact with an element as powerful as the wave. Are these merely the pompous ambitions of macho men and women, or is this a genuine path of exploration that one can enter by means of coming closer to nature?

Louis-Vincent Thomas points out in a section of his book on "transcending sexuality" that "great value is attached to 'natural love' insofar as it is capable of exercising a calming function and provoking metamorphoses."[31]

A slogan that often accompanies photos of tropical settings on postcards says "sex, sun, and sea." If one wanted to define surfing in concise terms, one could not do better than this. Not only in the world of surfing but everywhere where people are riding boards, the pleasures of sex are always evoked—the activities are compared. We see this in skateboard magazines as well as in snowboard magazines. Should we choose sex or riding? is the question the magazine *Snowboard Life* asked on the first page of its September 1996 issue, "Sex, Money, or POWDER?"

To make it clear that this whole business of the connection between surfing, transcendence leading to metamorphosis, and sex is not the mere product of an overly fertile masculine imagination, we need only consult once again Bessas's initiatory tale. There is a passage where the author is listening to an account being given by two of his friends, one of them a woman, after a particularly successful surfing session:

— "I don't understand it. I've been surfing for fifteen
years in every part of the world and never before have
I been in that state. I felt like I had become a medium.
The whole energy of the wave was transformed into
propulsive power by my board."

I tried to draw him out.

— "So, Ralph, you're discovering parapsychology in
surfing now?"

— "Don't be cynical, Yves. I'm telling you my body
actually became an electric wire that was capable of
capturing the energies of the sea and the sun. Those
forces were reinforced by the ones coming from you,
and all of them were transmitted together to the plastic
under my feet. But what was weird today was, there
were no parasites. There was no sense of collision—
I was like cradled by the wave."

— "Me too. I felt the same thing. It could be that the effort
we've been putting in over the last few weeks has
brought on this feeling of control, of ease, of freedom."

— "It's fantastic," said Linda. "I felt carried by you. At
one point, with the third wave, I had an orgasm."

— "You're exaggerating, Linda."

— "No, it's possible," Ralph said. "There's an obvious
connection between surfing and sexuality. Your

senses are so heightened that you can really reach the same state as when you are making love with a partner and you're completely synchronized with each other."[32]

Transformation and Death

When we look more at the image of the siren, it quickly becomes obvious that the siren represents something more than sexuality; this creature is first and foremost a symbol of death. According to Chevalier and Gheerbrand in their dictionary on symbolism: "She was made into an image of the dangers of sailing the sea and then into an image of death."[33]

For the surfer, reflection on death is inevitable in the face of waves several meters in height (some people surf waves of fifteen meters—fifty feet). The idea of one's own death, though generally anxiety-producing, can in exceptional cases be liberating. Since either "coming to grips" with death or thumbing one's nose at it can give birth to fear that limits the potential of transcendence, accepting death can be seen as a step in a process of initiation. It can be regarded as a test one must get through: "In certain works, it appears that the conquest of immortality is inseparable from a crude ordeal." A little farther on, the author adds the following:

> The ideal that man has pursued from time immemorial is to push back indefinitely the limitations of death, to live the longest possible time, not only by adding years to life but also by adding life to those years. The hero is no doddering or impotent old man, but an adult who is perpetually young.[34]

In the context of surfing, this idea is especially relevant, since remaining young, both in physical terms and in the sense of being awake to the present moment, is not only a desire but a probable outcome. If you consider the effort required to move in turbulent waters on a vehicle as fragile as a surfboard made of plastic foam laminated with fiberglass that is without any means of propulsion by motor or wind, it becomes clear that surfers have no choice but to remain youthful and physically fit if they want to stay alive.

Returning to the idea of the siren and the seductive and cruel sea, I would say that more than being an ordeal on the fantasy level with sexual connotations, resisting the siren is symbolic of an idealized individual confrontation, a passionate fundamental questioning on the part of a being who cannot conceive of death as a long process that is completely different from life, as a disappointing process in which one becomes a passive witness to the deterioration of the body, which is the vehicle of liberation. Ecstasy of the flesh is not the goal in this context but rather a means by which a mortal being is elevated by a taste of the eternity experienced beyond the joys of lovemaking or intense physical efforts. The experience of the tube, where the surfer is completely enveloped by the wave, leaving only one possible way out, is an almost psychedelic phenomenon that contributes to a conception of death of the sort that is particularly well expressed in the following passage:

> Those who have gone through death and rebirth
> sequences in their psychedelic sessions often describe a
> very radical change in their attitude toward death. Deep
> experiences of cosmic unity and of certain other
> transpersonal forms of consciousness seem to render the

fact of physical death irrelevant. . . . Those individuals who experienced the phenomenon of ego death followed by the experience of rebirth and cosmic unity seemed to show radical and lasting changes in their fundamental understanding of human nature and its relation to the universe. Death, instead of being the ultimate end of everything, suddenly appeared as a transition into a different type of existence. . . . [Those] who had transcendental experiences developed a deep belief in the ultimate unity of all creation.[35]

The experience of death/rebirth without leaving the physical body is one everyone has had at various moments at different levels of intensity. It can be brought on by things as simple as losing a job or a critical moment in a love affair that causes a sense of isolation, a loss of contact with what one imagines oneself to be. In any case, it is always an occult and mysterious experience. It is a miniature death.

Transcending the self, whether in a spiritual, sexual, or athletic context, brings this other dimension of the reality of death to life. An experiential inversion occurs: by consciously abandoning one-self to another being or to a force of nature, one feels one has redis-covered oneself.

The Immensity and the Minuteness of Nature

The oceans are so big, and when you take a moment to compare their size with that of the surfer, the surfer becomes insignificant, if not altogether invisible. Nonetheless humans manage through their activities to subject the sea to dangerous disruptions that are often irreversible, and they do it without the sense of respect they ought to feel on account of its immensity. Coastlines are changed to accommodate hotel development; pollutants are poured into the sea, and resources are overexploited, resulting in the relentless disturbance of an already precarious environmental equilibrium. This forces us to realize that even if, from the point of view of size, human beings are next to nothing, we nevertheless possesses a certain power of action.

What stands out here about surfers is that they use the energy of the sea without altering its nature. There is no consumption here but, rather, negotiation. At the worst, a surfer may be somewhat fanatical. This has led an anthropologist from the Université de la Réunion, Bruno Prochasson, to say that "the very nature of the practice of surfing invites us into or reveals to us a new relationship with the world."[36]

Prochasson reaches his conclusions in the context of contemporary astrophysics. As a "real departure in the history of the knowledge of the universe," astrophysics tells us that the universe is neither limited nor unlimited but simply in the process of growing; it is a succession of arrangements that are always different and therefore always richer in complexity. Here is how Prochasson applies this new insight to the example of surfing:

> Surfing seems to us to be an illustration, in the realm of sports, of this new approach to the world. An infinitesimal element when compared to the sea and its power, the surfer, as soon as he takes possession of a wave, dominates and organizes the movement that is there for his own purposes: he creates a more complex order.[37]

In this way the surfer in action is not only a metaphor for harmony but an example of the wholesome power of action, of creation and a way of being that is without harmful consequences. The surfer becomes an icon representing a responsible relationship with the environment. This is an icon that has been extensively exploited by a great number of organizations and businesses that are working to protect the environment or to stir up business in industries connected with outdoor activities.

The notion that the image of the surfer is a suitable vehicle for a contemporary reflection on human relationships with nature has been commented upon by Antoine Maurice, the author of a book on political activism and surfing. According to Maurice, ecologists and outdoor-activity enthusiasts—who share a sensibility we will talk about later—have revived a philosophical position the author attributes to Plato, a position that calls for human beings to act with modesty in their relationship with creation, an approach that promotes a sense of fullness. This outlook gives the subject the feeling of being a brother or sister of nature. The concept of Mother Nature is exchanged for that of Sister Nature, in connection with which Maurice says that "it's no longer up to nature to protect man but up to man to protect her, if he wants to assure his own salvation."[38]

If we are less pretentious and pay closer attention, perhaps we can come to see that between human nature and human culture, lots of different adventures are possible, and that destruction, often presented as the inevitable consequence of human action, is only too often just a lazy way to create wealth.

5 | Women Surfers

*E*ven though women have always ridden the waves with talent, there is no way around the fact that in the world of surfing, despite its praiseworthy values promoting freedom, man is often king. Surfing culture itself has remained unchanged despite the fact that the relationship between the sexes has undergone some changes since the time surfing was established in the West. Thus, even though surfing has a liberal image, what went on in California in 1960 was not the same as what went on in the days when men and women courted each other by surfing the same wave in Hawaii.

In the evolution of surfing, a separation of roles developed very quickly: it was the male as hero and the female as spectator, tanning on the beach in her scanty bathing suit. Of course there have always been as many women as men at the popular surfing spots, and the women have always appeared liberated, certainly on the level of dress, as they wandered about exposing most of their anatomy to the caresses of the air.

All the same, over the past few years, a new energy has been circulating among female surfers. We can see this in the specialist surfing media. Women first achieved acknowledgment by establishing themselves in the realm of snowboarding (where it is difficult to tell a male from a female). Then they were seen in films on boogie boards, and after that on surfboards. Finally the press and the magazines started taking an interest in this phenomenon. Of course, as I have already mentioned, women as an established force in surfing is not new. Although there have always been those women who have made their mark and left their influence on the history of surfing and on the world in general, it is only lately that they have freed themselves from a sometimes radical feminist movement whose demands they did not always understand. Women are working now to redefine a universe of their own for themselves in which they make plain (sometimes drawing unconsciously on the worthy accomplishments of the feminists) that they are determined to put an end to the pretensions of the male sex. This is what has been called "girl power," to pick up an expression used by the journalist Nadya Labi of *Time* magazine.[39]

There is a legendary female figure in the world of surfing whose story evokes the image of a woman who does what she likes, regardless of the risks involved in making waves in the hearts of men. We are talking about Ke-kai-o-Mamala, who was a chief of O'ahu (the ancient name of Waikiki), the capital of surfing in Hawaii, all through the beginning period of this sport. This woman was married to a shark fisherman by the name of Ouha, with whom she shared a peaceful existence of play and leisure.

Mamala was an aggressive surfer who had no fear of taking to the sea when the waves were massive and rolling in fast. Her reputation was widespread, and often a crowd came together on the beach to watch her exploits. One day a regional chief by the name of Honoka'upu saw her returning to shore and fell in love on the spot with this woman who, quite clearly, possessed extraordinary passion. The romantic power of this moment of encounter was not lost on Mamala, who left Ouha to marry the newcomer.

The cuckolded husband was very upset regarding his new position on life's discard pile and was deeply disturbed by the loss of his sweetheart. He made an attempt on Honoka'upu's life and tried to kill Mamala at the same time. He was captured, humiliated, and then thrown into the water at Ka-ihi-Kapu. Unable to tolerate the scorn-filled glances of the onlookers and insulted to the very core of his being, Ouha abandoned the human condition, a dimension too limited to express his growing rage and fury, and changed himself into a shark god, who to this day patrols the coast that runs from Waikiki to Koko Head. In Hawaii, the name of Mamala has continued to stand as that of the first radical female surfer, and her amorous adventures are still retold in a song called the "Mele of Honoka'upu."

Whether or not you believe in pairing up as a lifestyle, if you are interested in balance you will have to admit that this practice reaches its apex when the moment comes to surf as a couple. It is from this perspective, and toward a more equal weighting of the sexes in the surfing media, that the magazine *Surfing*, which is candidly masculine in its viewpoint, has tried for the last few years to add an annual supplement that talks a little bit about surfing women and their daily lives. The first go at this was a special "bathing suit" issue, which bore the name "Siren." There was no text, it was just beautifully illustrated. Still, it was noteworthy in the sense that for the first time readers of *Surfing* were able to gaze upon several women in action, facing breaking waves as they carved the surf at Puerto Escondido, taking positions on their boards as radical and stylized as any of the men.

In terms of editorial content, the effort was retooled for the second try, and this time the supplement was called *Surfing Girl*. Subtitled "Today and Yesterday," this edition was a sort of historical retrospective about women surfers of times gone by and served to highlight what their modern-day sisters were accomplishing. In this publication the sirens spoke in their own voices, signed articles, and put forth ideas related to the "girl power" movement. It was a little magazine that bore witness to the fact that women are increasingly making their presence felt in the world of surfing. "We're in an era of newfound female energy in surfing, where more and more girls are finding their way in the water," is a line from the editorial of this issue.

The third edition of *Surfing Girl* was a kind of hybrid affair, something halfway between a fashion magazine and a surfing periodical. There were a few articles, bathing suits came back to the fore, and the photographs were quite artistic. It was an iconographical study, representing dynamic women in a playful and refreshing context that had nothing to do with the "bathing suit issues" of the mass-distribution media, which are really not much more than soft-core pornography.

With the fourth issue, those responsible succeeded in presenting us with something fairly complete, and only the future will tell where this might lead. What we can say at the present is that from this point on, the women are here, a burgeoning presence but a real one, amid many challenges and the constant search for new paradigms. This is especially notable now that their queen is no longer with them.

Yes, the Hawaiian Rell Sun, "Queen of Makaha," died of cancer in 1998, after a battle with the disease that lasted for fifteen years. She was the principal female figure in surfing, always there in the documentaries and articles connected with women in love with the sea. Rell Sun was a surfer, a diver, a lifesaver, and a boater. She very justly bore the title "waterwoman." Her disappearance saddened a generation of young people whom she inspired and who quite simply adored her. Her talent for communicating the spirit of surfing and Hawaiian culture made her not only the number one ambassador of the ride but also eventually an official representative of the United States abroad. Rell Sun was a woman whose life was an adventure, a story of dreams come true, one after the other. She was born in 1950 and lived through much of the evolution of modern surfing. She always had a knack for bringing to life the connections that joined the traditional Hawaiian past with new developments in the world of surfing. Her own appearances were often made in conjunction with performances of traditional chants, and she often participated in cultural events and rites linked with the ocean. Rochelle Ballard, a professional woman surfer, described this exceptional woman in the following terms:

> For all the words that define the meaning of surfing, Rell
> is the expression of love and passion. . . . Rell has brought
> a wealth of Hawaiian aloha spirit to the sport of surfing.
> More than any other woman in the modern era, Rell has
> personified the idea of graceful, feminine surfing. A
> seminal figure in promoting professionalism and
> environmentalism, she has been a role model for women
> everywhere.[40]

An exemplary figure during her lifetime, Rell will surely remain an inspiring memory. Thanks to her, a way is now open, and looking at the amount of media coverage her death received, it is reasonable to believe that there is a very real desire to see such women in the world of surfing.

A Gremmie's Point of View

Situation: A young woman leaves her country with a girlfriend for a destination in the sunny part of the world. The objective is clear: to go see what these surfers look like in the flesh, because by reputation they are gorgeous hunks, "real men."

I propose here that we take a moment, making use of an interview that I did with one of these two young women, who is a friend of mine, to get to the bottom of what it is about surfers that stirs up so much desire. Let's find out what is at the source of this enchanting madness. So here is the essence of my conversations with a woman who got together with a Mexican surfer. The names, of course, are fictitious.

The two female friends land in Puerto Escondido, on the western coast of Mexico, find a hotel, and the following morning get up very early. At six, our two heroines are already in fine fettle. They've got their feet in the sand and they're gazing upon a stimulating spectacle—a horde of surfers, a bunch of virile guys swimming sexily out to the only thing that really turns them on, the waves. This transformative morning vision ended up prolonging by several months the young women's original plan for their Mexican vacation.

It was a confident, charismatic character with sculptured musculature by the name of Tazmael who seduced my friend Suzie, primarily on account of his knowledge of the sea and the comfort and ease of his relations with it. "When you discover the power of the waves, you develop respect for a person who confronts that power," Suzie told me. This surfer stood out through his mastery of the watery element and the exercise of his art, which took a very definite direction: "You guys think you're tough, but most of the time you have to bail out." So Tazmael distinguished himself physically, and then their relationship really began.

Suzie soon realized that he was a lifeguard as well as a surfer. Seeing Tazmael swimming in turbulent waters to save the lives of people he did not even know convinced her of his worth. "I saw him save two people. The people came over to thank him. I was really thrilled." Not only did her guy surf on a real board rather than a boogie board—which according to Suzie is distinctly less manly— but he surfed when the waves were big (in a place like Puerto Escondido, this means when the waves are bigger than five meters— sixteen feet). "On a second trip to Puerto, I went out on a boogie board, and I didn't feel the same power. And I got less of a charge out of seeing him go out on his body board—it was quite a bit less of a male thing."

During the six months Suzie spent with Tazmael in Mexico, he surfed nearly every day, and when they went together to visit his family in Vera Cruz on the eastern coast of Mexico, they both took advantage of the occasion to explore the waves of the Atlantic.

The man needed his surfing fix, and when he wasn't surfing, he worked a little bit and then rested. A man who spent a lot of time surfing was no problem for Suzie. "The fact that he needs to surf every day, I have less of a problem putting up with that than with a golfer. Why? I don't know, but it seems to me like a natural and normal activity."

She was fond of his rituals, the way he made the sign of the cross every time he went into the water, the sense of respect that was part of his attitude, and also the time he devoted to kissing her thoroughly before going out on his board. "I was sometimes torn between the desire to keep him with me and the desire to see him go off," she confided to me before talking about *her* experiences surfing, which ultimately were the clincher for her.

Suzie, instead of trying to keep her man at home in bed with her, also went surfing herself. Even though, at the beginning, she did not have a good understanding of the sea, it did not take long for her, reassured by the presence of her waterman, also to feel the desire for transcendence. Tazmael's presence gave her a sense of security, but Suzie discovered with time that her contact with the ocean was better when she was alone with it in the peaceful atmosphere of the setting sun. Quietly, the spirit of the surf took over, and curiously, her fears disappeared as it got dark. At the beginning her motivation was just to be able to say that she had tried, but then Suzie succeeded in making the experience her own and she began to get along quite well. I saw her—I ran into her on a surfing trip to Mexico—standing up on her board in the small waves of white foam, while I, in virile fashion, kept a lookout for the bigger waves and did not have the wisdom to capture the moment that she took advantage of so beautifully.

In addition to Tazmael's ability to perform on the board, it was his simplicity and his relaxed way of life that Suzie appreciated. The fact that he was satisfied with so little, that he was always barefoot, these were among the elements that made their life together something simple and satisfying. Suzie noted that sometimes, in spite of the very natural quality of the setting, there were very superficial aspects to the international social scene connected with surfing at Escondido.

Their experience together went through a much more intense period, and their relationship changed. Visiting Suzie at home in Quebec, Tazmael no longer had the power of the waves to tame him.

He no longer knew where or how to vent his energy. Several aspects of his personality melted away when he was in the city. Tazmael became a consumer, availing himself like everyone else of the artificial pleasures available there. He bought himself cool clothes and put his physical abilities to work in a rather shady way. He became a collector for a man who loaned money. Without the presence of the sea, he no longer represented the same thing for Suzie. She no longer saw the same beauty in the way he expressed power in his life.

Just as with Gidget, maybe Suzie's love was also really for surfing, and the sea. She had never missed the chance of seeing the sun setting over it—during her stay in Mexico, she had not missed it once. Suzie's admiration of Tazmael had also perhaps lessened after she had faced the power of the sea for herself and in this way got past the mythic quality of his relationship with it.

6 | The Social Scene

*T*he surfing world has its magazines, its competitive circuit, its heroes, and its horde of promoters. Each, in its own way, fuels the engine of the "sport." It is a milieu whose enthusiasts draw nourishment from so-called countercultural values: shared freedom, absence of a schedule other than that imposed by the sea, minimal consideration for technocratic laws, antiestablishment values, and so on.

The spirit of surfing informs a large social group, which goes far beyond avid practitioners. Surfing is the center of a sphere where some values evolve in one direction while others move in the opposite: sometimes the image of surfing is gentle and romantic, with a setting sun and surfers with magnificent smiles; sometimes it is warlike and violent, with illustrations of titanic waves that leave no room for refinement and delicate dance moves. These sometimes conflicting atmospheres generate diversity and evolution. Because opposing forces together create gravity, surfing remains in motion.

The surfing lifestyle, as I have just said, is one that appeals to lots of people beyond its devoted adepts. Also, prisoners of postmodernity, immured in alienating jobs or just in frustrating or unfruitful human relationships, idealize the lifestyle of surfing to the point of imagining it as something they will never be able to attain. True captives of determinism, they motivate surfers to revolt, to paddle harder against the wave of our conventional culture, which is already full of conditioned reflexes. What I am pointing to here is interaction: surfing challenges and creates desires. It is also challenged and desired itself. As a result, it remains prominent in the consciousness of the nonsurfing world.

This dynamic is true of all types of riding, as is attested by the refusal of the most accomplished snowboard professionals, such as Terje Haakonsen, to participate in the Olympic Games of Nagano (Japan). Nevertheless, snowboarding is a sport at the peak of its popularity. This boycott illustrates the fact that the world of riding is a universe where right-side-up and upside-down coexist. There is an urge for riders to remain pure, and at the same time to become popular figures and even millionaires (Haakonsen is a collector of actual gold ingots . . .).

Also at the Nagano games, Burton, the snowboard company, distributed T-shirts on which the famous Olympic rings were printed, but their interpretation depicted a series of interlocked handcuffs. This attitude shows the two poles in the world of riders: being and appearance, the natural and the artificial. Living in order to ride or riding in order to live? Many differing attitudes seem to flow from the ways this question can be answered.

Here once again, it is important remember that things are relative, for what we find in the very lucrative world of snowboarding, exists only in traces in the skateboarding world. And in the world of surfing, things are even more complex, given the nonreproducible character of waves. Even with the development of over-inflated styles in the professional surfing circuit, it remains impossible to guarantee that a suitably commercial demonstration—or even a competition—will take place. This situation invites us into deeper reflection concerning the exploitation of this resource and begs us to take an ethical position on the matter of competitive surfing.

This is why surfing will remain a source of inspiration for generations in search of freedom and will long represent the archetype of an outright revolutionary way of life, especially when compared with the materialistic dream of ranch house complete with lawnmower, a thousand-and-one household appliances, and the inevitable automobile. Not that surfing is a social model in itself, but its relationship to the unpredictable natural world prevents its evolution from following a straight path governed by laws—of nature or otherwise.

From One Extreme to the Other

I now return to my effort, to my desire, to talk about the attraction and the resistance at the heart of the matter. There is a mysterious force that maintains the spirit of surfing, so that it doesn't dissipate with time any more than it implodes.

Orbiting around the values and images of the ocean, as well as a passion for it, the world of surfing contains ideas that are completely opposed to each other, just as the earth itself does, with its opposing poles. The two poles of surfing, which nourish the fundamental paradoxes of its social universe, are none other than creation and destruction—just like the rising of a wave and its crash. We could both rejoice in a wave's appearance as well as cry over its impermanence. While some people lament a wave's breaking, others rejoice at seeing a bigger one or a gentler one come into existence. Such is the world of surfing, since it is human—in the same place that some see evil, others see good.

On a more concrete and less philosophical level, I want to stress that in the world of surfing there is no fundamental or completely dominant outlook. It is more a case of ideas that are sometimes complementary, sometimes conflicting, that are caught up in a pattern of relationship that both creates and perpetuates change.

First there is the vision of the surfer who sees herself as a creator, who sees the wave as her accomplice when she executes a radical cutback on its lip, throwing off a fan-shaped swath of spume, a million droplets hurled toward the bright sky, toes wide apart, bearing witness with her entire being to the will to exist, allowing a refined form of the art to emerge on the spot.

Then there is the surfer who sees the wave as the hand of the enemy, as a weapon that destroys life. For this kind of surfer, the wave is dangerous: it must be conquered, dominated, even annihilated beneath his board, which is unleashed on the wave like an avalanche. Between these two extremes there is diversity, multiplicity, and as many attitudes as there are individual personalities.

There is no method nor is there a clear set of categories for classifying all attitudes and all surfers. Each one is unique. Thus we cannot always say that such and such a surfer is to be completely associated with a given current of thought or a particular approach.

A surfer with an aggressive style who takes on a wave in a radical way and works close to the reefs is not necessarily a person who will contribute toward a competitive form of the sport. This might just be a surfer who loves the intensity and the sensations and has no desire to see their development evaluated. By the same token, it would be impossible to say that any adept of the free ride is completely original, untouched by any external influence, impervious to the actions of others and to the judgments and appreciations of which he or she might be the object. All humans define themselves in part in relation to reality—in relation to nature, culture, the force of the elements, and other living beings. Human beings contain an element (doubtless in varying degrees) that is derived from other people.

The awakening of a sense of existence, which simply allows one to feel that one is alive, is perhaps what all people who practice surfing have in common. This is equally true for any human being who perceives the present in an intense way, who takes ultimate pleasure in each instant of life.

Contact with the power of the wave, with the accumulation of kinetic energy in its lower part, which is vented when you make a bottom turn—this is another thing that all surfers might well have in common. But the way they relate to this sensation is personal. The resource is accessible to everybody—the energy that is carried by that which is in movement or alive, but the movements that follow contact with this energy become an individual matter. Sometimes the response is spiritual, sometimes superficial, and it cannot be homogenized, controlled, trivialized, or reduced to uniformity. There are as many routes and pathways through the movements of humanity as there are people to trace them. It is the same thing in the world of surfing—a matter of plurality.

If it is impossible to categorize individuals, it is possible to identify certain attitudes without classifying them hierarchically, to identify ideals and to see tendencies taking form in the surf. I will not attempt to define all the social orientations present in the universe of surfing, which would be a temporally infinite challenge. I will instead depict here a few profiles presented in the mass-market literature and the specialized media and also based on what I have been able to see for myself in my experiences in the field. The point I wish to highlight here is that there are many worlds of surfing.

Any reductionist tendency that would seek to diminish the unique manifestation of surfing to a mere sport would be the proof of major ignorance. Sport, as defined by adversity, combat, and struggle with an adversary, is only observable in a surfer paddling on the board. Once standing and moving onto the shoulder or into the tube of a wave, the surfer is dancing:

> Because in the heart of every surfer—young, child, man, woman, thin, fat, kook, pro—there lives a lover who yearns to tango, not wrestle. Surfing is the dance. But paddling, with all its prerequisite athleticism—the straight-forward approach, repetitive movement and quantifiable results—is the sport.[41]

The practice of surfing, whether in the athletic dimension or the emotional manifestation, remains fascinating because it is a brilliant illustration of the interaction of the forces of the universe. In concentrating the energy provided by the wave to accelerate, the surfer displays all the creative potential of resistance versus attraction—the motivating force of life.

The Opposite of the Conditional Approach

The sea has no schedule; it must be taken when it offers itself. It has its moods, and it is the surfer who must yield and accommodate them. This is very different from navigating our service-oriented society, in which you can order anything you want and if the delivery is late, you pay nothing. This is why it is often difficult for non-surfers to form an accurate idea about the ambiance of surfing. Traditional Western values and the idealized surfing lifestyle seem to be thousands of miles apart. Whether they have no access to the sea or because they are incapable of deciding just to go ahead and do it, people who are fascinated by surfing all too often ride only in their imagination, conceiving of a paradise where everything is allowed and nothing is as monotonous as it seems to be in real life. Like many manufactured icons, the image of the surfer seems designed to serve as a projection of fantasies of both the lowest vices and the greatest of human aspirations.

Filled with prohibitions and taboos, the world of surfing seduces and shocks at the same time. Matt Warshaw, a reporter for *Surfer's Journal*, made reference in the third issue of the magazine in 1997 to a comparison (put forward at the end of the 1960s in *Time* magazine), that illustrates well the ambivalence—the coveted, almost illegal side of the thing: "Riding a board through the surf is a little like going on hashish."[42]

Seen from the outside, surfers do what they like. They walk almost nude on the beach, do not have any appointments, and after surfing, they calmly smoke a joint. If every myth contains its element of reality, the opposite is also true. Frequently, life having somehow caught up with them, surfers one day find themselves face-to-face with a choice. For Warshaw this choice fundamentally belongs to a context of existential questions raised by Daniel Duane and William Finnegan, two authors who have written about surfing. This choice, presented in the form of a question, can be formulated as simply as: Is it possible to remain a surfer while maintaining a career? In answer to this question, Warshaw provides a balanced case in point:

How, for example, does an educated and ambitious person split his time between surfing and serious work? Finnegan's answer: it can't be done. He follows his ambition and moves from San Francisco to New York. (Writer Duane, responding to the same question, says it can be done, follows his ambition and moves—with a full quiver of boards—from Santa Cruz to San Francisco.)[43]

Another question that arises, beyond the life plans of particular people and their individual ideals, is this: Are there still wild surfers who couldn't care less about what people might say about them, who are exclusively tuned in to what helps them to be happy and fully concentrated on what the waves might bring them?

Philosophies of the Ephemeral

Philosophy, in brief, is a trial balloon, an effort on the part of human beings trying to give some meaning to their existence. From the sparest simplicity to a level of complexity that boggles the mind, philosophies are formed in the image of those who construct and create them.

At the root of all action and any doctrine, whether compensatory or repressive, there is a hint of philosophy, a guiding motivation that makes possible a balance between the finite and the dizzying infinite. Sometimes the limits of reason are forgotten, the mind having decided to give them the slip, and a transition takes place, a passage from reality to mirage. At that point the rational bases of philosophy dissipate and stories and tales arise that allow madness to be productive. Nevertheless, even if they are not pure products of reason, what we call mythologies or popular cosmologies still have their value, because between reason and intuition lie visions. In brief, to have a philosophy is a bit like believing in a story that is personal to us, in some sense, simply having a vision of life.

Why would surfers think up philosophies that are particularly suited to them, and what is it about them that might be unique? In fact, philosophies, in spite of the diversity of ideas found in them, always have their human origins in common. Though surfing might lend itself to the development of a certain kind of questioning, at the same time there are other human beings in all sorts of other situations who are haunted by similar reflections. Thus many master thinkers, in spite of having followed different pathways to get there, have ended up with the same conclusions at the end of their lives. As witness to this, let us consider this statement of Zen scholar D. T. Suzuki, regarding the thought of a great German philosopher of the thirteenth century:

> When I read Meister Eckhart, I have the impression of reading a Buddhist text transposed into a different terminology; but as far as inner understanding is concerned, the two views are identical. This kind of understanding corresponds to intuition.[44]

In addition, though the range of philosophical approaches related to surfing is considerable, it is possible to discern that these ideas, while differing in presentation, form a broad system of interrelated thoughts. And it is even possible to observe that, in certain contexts and for certain people, there is quite simply an absence of any philosophy at all in their practice of surfing.

As a physical activity capable of nourishing the mind and spirit in many ways, surfing (and riding in general) is an open door, a treasure that is at first hidden within the surfer rather than at the bottom of the sea. It is realistic to think that not all surfers have discovered this treasure and conceived of a philosophy that takes it into account. In fact, there are many stories where heroes go off on a crusade, embark on a journey to find out what really makes them vibrate inside, only later to realize that all through the quest, they were already sitting on what was desired so much, the very thing they were dreaming of flushing out of its hiding, or perhaps of finding again. To become aware of the link that unites a person with the sea, sometimes the surfer must lose it in order to desire it, must detach from it so as to be free of the idea of possession or deprivation and internalize the experience of the wave.

Gentle Warriors and the Quest for the Center

> The ocean is constantly present in me; I never feel any separation. Surfing is a form of martial art, a discipline of the mind, the body, and the soul. On the sea, you have to be fierce, fast, and violent, fluid and serene as she is. At that point you become one with the ocean.
> —Brian Keaulana, Hawaiian surfer

It is through the holes they pierce in reality that adventurers and warriors navigate into new and different spaces. Rich in experiences lived through in the nearness of death, they have ended by taming death, demythologizing it, and they have clearly understood that death exists only to give flavor to life. They seek intensity in unity, concentrating on the center, the famous point of balance that allows them to ride in any direction. These individuals believe that there is a connection between the actions they take and the adventure they live.

Practicing riding as an art, the surfers I am speaking of here do not do what they do primarily for money. This is certainly not what you see when you try to figure out how they earn a living. You do not find them in factories, you find them on the beach. They must live "from love," like Zachary Richard;[45] at least that is the understanding you come to if you believe what the surfer Kahea Hart says: "Money does grow on trees, you just have to know where to look. That's a big problem in this world, people don't look at what nature provides."[46]

Though their bellies are always full, these people do not accumulate much fat. They are in exceptional physical condition and seem to be in harmony with everything that is natural. Some people call them soul surfers.

Endowed with a soul that is riding, with an attitude very much directed toward what the present has to provide, they are not concerned with what is going on behind the scenes: competitions, glorious trips, and tales of passion on the move. They are discreet, masters in other realms as well as on the earth. They are heart surfers. They are happy.

To perpetuate traditions without hanging on to rigid political and cultural frameworks, to translate art by means of the act, to sublimate speech so as to listen only to the music of sounds, to empower all sensations—this is the spirit of their mission. In Hawaii, the holy land of surfing if there is one, surfing is full of messages, flows of information coming from surfers who are fools and sages: "Surfing there is charged with meaning. It is part of the culture, it participates in the myths and legends, it is not only a physical teaching, but also an emotional and spiritual one."[47]

The soul surfers feed a continuum whose presence owes more to movement than to time. This is a tradition that lives and breathes on the basis of a very concrete practice, a contact with impermanence that is constantly being renewed, a relentless reminder of the unique and irreproducible character of each instant.

There is no getting around the link between this attitude toward surfing and the Eastern traditions of Zen and Taoism: two hymns to the present and to action. This is an attitude that Gerry Lopez, a Hawaiian surfer of Japanese and German-Cuban origin whom I mentioned earlier, sums up in very simple terms: "Many people can anticipate or remember, but the most important thing is to know how to place your foot, here and now."[48]

Between Two Bodies of Water

There are surfers who are socially and philosophically engaged, and there are those who are much more inclined simply to drop out. The latter group is large in number, young, composed of protestors against the American Dream, without the principal supporters of this dream even being aware of them and their concerns. Yet what is more widespread at this point, it seems, than dissatisfaction with this dream? These young rebels are bold enough to believe that the establishment is the sole reason that misfortune is permanent and happiness no more than a hollow illusion; however, what they call the system never sees their point of view at all. As they grow older, new escapes (surfing, the circus, basketball, skateboarding, or collecting butterflies) replace the bonbons of childhood. This escape mode can also mutate into crack addiction, nasty ambitions, or an all but organic connection with television.

They flee, while at the same time abandoning themselves in an almost conformist fashion to a path too often inappropriately called revolution. Rejecting convention and the dictatorship of education as a matter of principle, they live as best they can on the leftovers of disorder and the unusual, engaging whatever is different to such a degree that they normalize it.

But one original source comes to the fore when they leave the social realm behind to become one with the animal within themselves, their physical movements attaining the high level of their ideals, of their greatest dreams. You can see them pivoting and executing forms that are so self-evident and spontaneous that it is difficult to imagine, even when these maneuvers are very daring ones, how they could be done otherwise. Feeling yourself in movement, having the sense that you have to act in order to feel the life in you, dodging discussions on the apparent inevitabilities of progress and all the other questions that are just too heavy: these are the strengths and weaknesses of adolescents.

These young people are powerful because they have the conviction, too often forgotten by adults, that they can change everything, and this is why they often provoke reactions. With their fresh, active approach, they incite fear, great fear, in the entrenched members of the middle class. You have to have seen skateboarders exercising their art on a ramp to grasp what I am trying to convey here. It is the idea that each young person has, hidden within, an unimagined treasure, a unique resource that can be transformed into dynamic spirals allowing him or her, on skateboard or surfboard, to spin in all directions, now and again coming to a halt, pausing to breathe a good lungful of the air he or she has just been flying in.

This image of a social offender, this little mutant who suddenly goes wild, has been picked up by a number of surfing enterprises for advertising. Volcom, one of these companies, presents the most radical copy in this regard: "Youth against establishment. The Establishment: An exclusive or powerful group that controls or strongly influences a government, society, or field of activity." In the ad where this short text appears, one sees a teenager bounding out of the city in a pose verging on the splits, naked to the waist, hair flying in the wind, raising his middle finger to the sky with one hand, while his other points downward to the ground and backward. On the ground there is a radio, a very small backpack, a surfboard, a skateboard, and a snowboard. The ultimate triad. The ad also shows a few riding scenes in a montage that brings in a variety of rather punk and retro images. It is an extreme symbol for young people espousing these ideals, spitting on society, believing they can turn their back on it forever.

Another ad, this time from Kik Wear Industries, shows a sort of village priest or parson, Bible in his hand, face-to-face with a lineup of youths whom a voluptuous secretary is asking to disrobe. The parson, with his free hand, tosses the youths' pants into a metal drum to burn while the starry American flag floats behind the scene, high above. The clothing that gets burned is clearly the company's product and the attitude of the young people who are deprived of it is that of defiant rebels. An amusing scene, a caricature of the control exercised by the old puritans over the young members of their society, in which the extremes miraculously succeed in coexisting.

In the literature of adventure, a fellow named Jeff Spicoli (from the film, *Fast Times at Ridgemont High*) is the archetype of youth. His creator, Cameron Crowe, writing for *Rolling Stone* magazine, presented him in 1981 in the following terms:

> He spoke thickly, like molasses pouring from a jar. Most every school morning Spicoli awoke before dawn, smoked three bowls of marijuana from a small steel bong, put on his wetsuit, and surfed before school.[49]

But despite all that, over time, many teenagers pull themselves back together, sometimes encouraged by one of the rare adults who is committed to young people or by some species of gift within them that allows them to give birth to wholesome ambitions. Those who were believed lost reconcile themselves with the grownups and finally begin cultivating the talents they possess. Sometimes these talents frighten them a good deal, because changing the world when you have the feeling you really can do it is a very heavy weight on one's mind and conscience.

Riding, for the young people who cannot see any place for themselves in the social vision of their times, gives them a chance to get a taste of who they are, to wander freely in a world that has made a conveyor-belt factory out of the formal educational process, unfortunately abandoning personal realization in favor of an alienating conformism that facilitates the servitude of the individual to a system that he or she eventually ends up being dependent upon. Claudia Paccagnini, an Italian psychologist and teacher, comments on this in a work she published on skateboarding at the time it was beginning to flourish in France:

> Skateboarding gives children an opportunity to assert themselves in a society that tends to make little puppets out of them. It helps them to externalize and release their potential for exhibitionism. It allows them in addition to fight against the constraints of the city and to evolve freely outside the overwhelming and repressive context of school and family. These chains that weigh upon them, especially in the United States, have provoked a tidal wave of liberation that is easy to understand.[50]

The Slide into Crime

Those who do not come back from their sojourn on the margins often cultivate a kind of couldn't-care-less attitude and sometimes fall outright into the world of crime, fantasizing about the big caper that will allow them to move freely in the world, to follow the waves around the world without having to worry about paying the bills.

There is a widely distributed film that gives a good picture of the way of life in these closed circles, surfer clans that have gone the way of crime. Titled *Point Break*, it features Keanu Reeves and Patrick Swayze, as well as Anthony Kiedis, lead singer of the the Red Hot Chili Peppers. The film's plot revolves around a series of daring bank robberies perpetrated by a group who wear masks featuring former American presidents. A veteran cop attributes these crimes to a gang of surfers, owing to the effectiveness of the robbers, their control of space, and especially their unique signature: one of the presumed surfers exposes his buttocks to the bank cameras, showing the words "Thank You" inscribed just below his tan line. The heavy tan, the cohesion of the group, and a few other clues lead the seasoned old cop and the new recruit who is his assistant (Keanu Reeves) to infiltrate a gang of surfers, with whom Reeves comes to share real friendship. Patrick Swayze, who plays the chief of the gang, is extremely charismatic in his role of guru of the free ride. With his explanations of Zen and his teachings on surfing, he succeeds in piercing Reeves's armor. Reeves finds his convictions as a lawman and righter of wrongs cutting loose and beginning to drift. This is a film in which the two poles of surfing discussed earlier are well depicted. It shows clearly that involvement in the practice of surfing can flow sometimes from a desire to create, sometimes from a desire to destroy.

A Taste for Ecology

Whether surfers are philosophers, dropouts, or robbers, it is the wave that allows them, through a process in which they can influence the outcome and therefore are able to feel that they exist, to escape from the meaninglessness of industrial death, from the result of a life without excitement or passion, regulated by the tempo of modern production.

Surfers flee the chemical and social pollution to ride, like a pure waveform, in harmony with a natural world that gives them the courage to face the things they find too difficult. But in a moment of history in which the word *evolution* has strangely become a synonym of *devastation*, they now have to face the fact that sometimes civilization beats them to the beach, and they see that what they were running away from has prevailed and is killing the love of their life:

> Have you ever taken a stroll in the area of Bilbao, that industrial hell worthy of the Third World? All those toxic factories are planted at the edge of the sea. . . . It has to be said: even in a polluted sea there will always be waves to surf. . . . Sure, but who wants to make love to a corpse?[51]

This account gives a very accurate sense of the bitterness and disgust felt by many members of the world community of surfing who, as they pass beyond the insurrectional phase of adolescence, sometimes transform their rebellion into meaningful action.

Occasionally it does happen that the little delinquent turns into a militant adult.

Urban sprawl is going full speed ahead on all fronts, and it is clear that tomorrow will offer fewer beautiful spots to surf than we have today. A shoreline reshaped, waters filled in to expand a coastal area so that it can be developed and the burger lovers can come there to get their tans, and the next thing you know the sea bottom is no longer playing its part so well. The waves do come, but they hardly break. This is often what happens when there are major developments along the shoreline. The tall buildings block the winds coming off the land and change the way the elements interact at the surface of the sea. The trade in coral (prohibited in the United States, even though import is permitted) destroys the best surfing spots, because the coral reefs are the ideal obstacle needed for shaping the big breakers. On top of this, the pollution caused by factories and the accursed lawn fertilizer industry (the herbicides and pesticides get into the ground water and invariably end up in the sea) make surfing dangerous because of the skin ailments they can cause.

In the midst of this grim picture, however, a group of people with their hearts and minds full of ideals make their appearance. These are the members of the Surfrider Foundation. This is a nonprofit group whose members work peacefully to reverse the pollution of shore areas and oceans through various educational, conservation, and research projects. Composed initially of surfers, the foundation also came to include other riders (snowboarders mainly) in its team ranks. Thanks to this new blood, the Snowrider project was born, the goal of which is to sensitize snow enthusiasts—snow is also made of water—to the problems of the environment. This is a major organization whose opinion counts. The proof was the participation of Darryl Hatheway, representative of the Capitol Hill chapter, at the first White House Environment Day celebration on June 6, 1996. In the December issue of *Surfing* magazine of that same year, this environmental activist could be seen shaking hands with the American president. In the course of the day, Bill Clinton made a speech in which he enthusiastically highlighted the committed activity of this environmental organization.

There are other examples like this foundation. For instance, there is Tavarua Island—a Pacific island whose main mission is to welcome surfers from all over the world while at the same time encouraging its local people to participate in a development process that respects their traditions and environment. This shows that the surfing world is an independent entity that has developed a social and environmental conscience of its own, reflecting the values found in the practice of surfing.

Small-Time Politics and Localism

Though surfing is very much an individual activity, surfers do often organize themselves into clans. Certain members of these clans acquire a special status because they have a talent for weather prediction or just because they have charisma. Otherwise, the main factor in creating the hierarchies of these clans is technical competence. Of course, in addition there are matters of seniority, and in certain places, localist considerations.

Flowers in their hair, a superrelaxed attitude, a satisfied and jovial smile—these qualities and accoutrements might mislead you to think that surfers cannot sometimes be combative and terribly territorial. For all that, surfers remain human beings, and they struggle and quarrel over things that many people would consider trifling. They are governed by rules and prohibitions just as they are as public citizens, and amid the fervid and sometimes nearly hysterical environment created when the waves are of epic proportions, you have to be politically skillful to survive, since the code you are living by often functions on an unspoken level. Sometimes even innocent beginners have to learn the hard way; for all they can do to protect themselves, they may still wind up with a surfboard or a fist in their mouth.

On each site, things work differently, though in a way well known to the locals. The challenge for the newcomer is always to adapt. In certain places there are kings, guys who enjoy special treatment. They are given priority. They have the right to choose the waves they want because of their past successes and their reputation. In other places everything comes down to how big your biceps are. If a visitor is ready to confront the toughest muscle guys among the locals, then he will have no problem surfing. Many spots are a jumble of miscellaneous small-time politics where anybody, from the veteran to the novice, can make his or her own laws.

You may face different receptions, but the political stake in play is always the same: access to the waves. Impassioned obsession together with some form of reasoning has resulted in a number of schools of thought that have been devised to determine who has priority of access to a given wave. Sometimes consideration is given to the position of the surfer in the lineup or, considering the surfer's abilities, what chances he or she might have to make good use of the wave. All this is negotiated in silence, and action replaces discussions that might become too long.

Much of the time, out in the water, there is no hostility. But good-wave days are limited, and at certain moments the struggle to enjoy the resource becomes very tense. This would be true even without taking into account the fact that the number of surfers is continually growing, thanks in part to a surfing industry that keeps coming up with new toys for riding.

At the seaside, amid the ordinary bathers, body boarders, and other amateurs of the ride, surfers have developed the reputation of being predators, primarily because a surfer's vehicle can also serve as a weapon. The nose end of a surfboard can function like a ram's horn when it smashes into the body of a swimmer or a rider whose face is at water level, as the body boarder's is.

Thus localism is a somewhat summary and off-the-cuff process that consists of terrorizing, intimidating, or assaulting all intruders who venture into a place to which the local surfers have decided to close off access. Zorba, a surfer interviewed in *Surfer* magazine, puts razor blades on the end of his surfboard, while his buddies are content with destroying the cars of people who come from too far away. A variety of techniques, all with the same goal: when outsiders are spotted, make sure they lose any desire they might have had to assert themselves.

Gloom and Doom and Outright Terror

The fear dimension of surfing, producing a confusing atmosphere, is mainly fed by horror literature like that produced by the author Kem Nunn (*Tapping the Source*, *Dogs of Winter*). It is, of course, easy to imagine spectacular accidents involved with surfing and to suspect criminality in every tattooed figure strolling the beach, but we must also consider that if the world of surfing were such a tough one, so full of crooks, it would not enjoy all the prestige it does as a result of its associations with values such as freedom, contact with nature, and that rare thing, personal realization.

The vision of the surfing world as a dark and macabre place is derived from the same workings of the imagination as those that produce horror films and literary works in which murders are committed with chainsaws and shovels. It is the work of an industry devoted to mass consumption that takes advantage of surfing as a source of exotic scenarios.

Of course aggression is an integral part of surfing, just as it is always present in one form or another in any very dynamic activity in which a great deal of energy is expended.

A relevant example, although a subtle one, is the advertisement of the company No Fear that was printed on the back cover of an American surfing magazine. It contains this message: "Water. In theory you can breathe it . . . but just once." The accompanying image shows three boards floating in the water without their surfers, drifting at the foot of a gigantic wave, abandoned beneath a darkening sky. There is nothing here to recall sunshine or evening gatherings by the fire. This sort of publicity is, however, rare, and though we do find ads or articles in specialized magazines depicting surfers who have been more or less mutilated—an eye gouged out by the very pointed end of a surfboard or an arm cut open to the bone in the course of a nocturnal escapade—as I have already pointed out, it is primarily in magazines intended for mass consumption that one finds these horror stories where the heroes are surfers.

From the surfing magazines that show a bit of blood to the dark fiction of Kem Nunn, we find a range of tales that chill and thrill. Is this a bad thing? Is it a good thing? First of all, we have to remember that it is often no more than imagination. However, you do occasionally run across a true story of someone who escaped death in the water. These stories are always gripping, because they are rare and disturbing. Here is a stimulating passage taken from an article by Ken Doudt, a surfer who was caught by a great white shark off Cannon Beach in Oregon:

> Suddenly I heard a kind of muffled growl. I felt something huge and massive taking hold of my back while something else crushed my rib cage, breaking my ribs. A fraction of a second later, I was being dragged toward the bottom. . . . I twisted like an eel trying to pull myself loose while at the same time hammering the beast's head with my fist. I expected to see my legs floating next to me at any moment. The shark tried to drag me down for a third time. Without success. He leaped out of the water and shook me like a dog would a bone, with such violence that I was sure my last hour had arrived. . . . I found myself alone amid pools of blood about a hundred meters from the beach. Terrified, my eyes searched for the shark. Where was he? I was sure he was going to strike again. . . . My ribs had torn through my flesh, exposing my organs. With each beat of my heart, blood oozed from my torn arteries. The pool of blood was only partly contained by my shredded wetsuit. . . . The roar of a siren approaching renewed my courage. *I was saved.*[52]

This story is exceptional because these things do not happen often, even though people get a kick out of saying that the surfer on his board casts the same shadow as the eared seal that is the favorite

113

food of the great white sharks and that for this reason surfers get themselves eaten. The author of the story above recognizes himself as having been negligent in continuing to surf despite at least three warning signs that indicated to him that there was a shark in the area. For those of you whose appetites were not satisfied by the excerpt above, I recommend a book by Greg Ambrose, *Shark Bites— True Tales of Survival*, a collection of stories of people from Kauai, Maui, Oahu, California, and the Pacific Islands, who were attacked by sharks. This is a work in which the author tries to replace with respect the fear that many lovers of the wave and the beach have for those creatures who come to us from another age, unpredictable and silently dangerous.

As to the eternal question of whether or not there might be sharks in such and such a place where you would like to go surfing, it is a question that should never be asked. There might be sharks anywhere there is salt water. The belief that there are more sharks where the water is warm is a myth. In Forillon National Park on the Gaspé Peninsula of northern Quebec, a large white shark that was captured there is on exhibit.

All the same, there are southern seas where the shark is king. Like any other animal, the main occupation of this large cartilaginous fish is finding food. I spoke above of the eared seal, but there are other seals, dolphins, mollusks, and tortoises of which sharks are also extremely fond. So it is in an environment rich in food and oxygen—thus in relatively cold waters, because there is more oxygen in cold water and thus more food—that the shark hunts. Should you be frightened? Only about 10 percent of sharks are potentially dangerous to humans; some sharks feed only on plankton. In all these stories of nasty sharks and nice fish, one thing is really certain—the fear of sharks is out of proportion to the number of surfers who have served as their feast.

Since we are speaking of this sort of thing, I will share an anecdote that was recounted by Jorge, the person in charge of a nature park in Puerto Rico, who told me this story, recounting one of several encounters with sharks during his thirty years of surfing. The first visit was over quickly. The shark approached and came very close to him and a small group of friends and then swam away without hesitation. They were spared because his companions knew the shark, a pal of theirs from the neighborhood. This is the kind of story that I know you had to be there to believe, but it's Jorge's story, and he believes it. But the encounter did not prevent him from surfing, any more than he is intimidated by the idea that he might run into a shark right now. This is an attitude shared by many surfers of the past. The Duke, when he was coming out of the water one time in Australia after having given a surfing exhibition in a spot infested by sharks, responded to the onlookers who asked him if he had seen any of the predators: "Sure, plenty."

"They didn't bother you?"

"No, and I didn't bother them either."[53]

Artists of the Ride

A good number of surfers, independent of the surroundings that nourish them, have a deep artistic sensibility. A simple piece of paper, the body of a Volkswagen minibus, broken surfboards (about which there are many stories to tell), these are some examples of the surfaces that surfers enjoy painting or texturing, a gesture of offering some impression of the visions the sea has just inspired in them.

Beverly Decker, an American who grew up in the American surf culture of the 1950s and 1960s, makes custom furniture and various art objects with bits of surfboards, fins, and other surfing artifacts. Seth Quinby paints incredible pictures in which the representation of curves and movement have no equal other than the feeling that takes hold of a man or woman who is actually surfing. These people have made art their profession, but when you are around people who surf, you quickly find that they all create some form of art, more or less developed, even if it is just the curves they describe on the water, the ultimate canvas on which surfers can express their feelings, their joy in life, a manifestation of the power of the present moment. Without doubt, the surfing world produces this kind of flowing and magical art because it is inspired by the sea, the source of life. This results in a variety of styles full of curves and cosmic explosions.

In the context of art, surfing literature—a worthy art form and an excellent cultural vehicle—fully holds up its end. From the first poetic and liberated lines by a surfer named Lord Byron in 1817 (*Childe Harold*), many a page has been printed that aims at doing justice to the pleasures of the ride. The great Jack London had a go at it. After surfing for a few days at Waikiki, he composed a short story for the pages of *Woman's Home Companion*, which four years later became one of the chapters in his book *The Cruise of the Snark*. This book made it possible for the first time in history for the public at large to discover what London called "a royal sport for the natural kings of the earth." It's nothing less than that.

London's writings and those of other authors such as Mark Twain and Frederick O'Brien were influential factors as far as the romantic image associated with surfing in the twentieth century is concerned. These authors provided more than just simple observations. They delivered accounts of the practice, the initiatory experiences, and the way of life connected with surfing. These writers, by involving themselves in the activity itself and in the community of surfing, produced accounts that became lasting reference points: "O'Brien is happily integrated with the local surfers. He can nonetheless observe with an anthropological eye."[54]

Many other works followed that contributed to the spread and evolution of surfing culture up to the present period. Among the books it would be good to have a look at if you are enthusiastic about surfing, I would highlight the following: *Gidget* by Fredrick Kohner (a series of films was also made on the basis of this novel), *Playing Doc's Games* by William Finnegan, *You Should Have Been Here an Hour Ago* by Phil Edward, and *Caught Inside* by Daniel Duane.

Although it can be expressed on canvas or paper, sculpted, translated into verse or described in a novel, ultimately the spirit of surfing and the fullness of its artistic dimension can be manifested only in the practice of surfing itself. Truly, it is enough to savor the profundity of the movements, the intensity, the presence and simplicity of surfers such as Donavon Frankenreiter, Kahea Hart, or Shea Lopez—and I could name many other known and unknown surfers—to wax to the full one's desire to be exposed to this spontaneous and natural art that arises directly from contact between the sea and a human mind. This about says it all regarding the originality and uniqueness of surfing photography. These photographs leave no one indifferent, and this is why they are used, often without a direct connection to the subject matter, in so many advertisements. A man or a woman standing up inside a blue tunnel penetrated by light and a pattern of circular lines, evolving out of the water like a god or a goddess, arising from nowhere and heading directly toward the camera lens—this is one of the most dynamic of photographic subjects. Photographic artists do not hesitate to submit themselves to the rocking of the waves, using all manner of waterproof equipment in order to capture from just the right angle the transparency of the water, the effect of the setting sun spreading on the glasslike surface of a wave. Some go as far as making it possible to share the appreciative perspective of fish by taking pictures underwater with the lens directed upward.

The last aspect of this section on art is about music. Obviously, the rhythm of music is part and parcel of the social universe of the surfing world. And it was not just yesterday that the Hawaiians began expressing their love of the sea in song, that they began taking the time to celebrate harmoniously the gifts of the wind, communicating with nature through the expressiveness of their instruments and chants. This culture of music passed beyond the Hawaiian Islands as surfing culture spread to the entire globe. We have only to think of the Beach Boys, Jane's Addiction, Pearl Jam (Eddie, the lead singer, is a surfer, and the band is the most important patron of the Surfrider Foundation), as well as all of the California punk groups who provide the beat for young people these days, to see that the influence of surfing on music has not been just a passing fashion.

Rock groups sing about surfing, but there are also surfers who rock. Kelly Slater, five-time champion surfer of the world, and Rob Machado, a legendary surfer whose style shows an incredible flexibility, produced their first disk, *Songs from the Pipe*, on the prestigious Epic label in 1998. Other surfers, such as Corky Carroll, Tom Curren, and Donovan Frankenreiter, have also recorded CDs, and the

Surfrider Foundation has put two collections with big-name singers on the market in an effort to raise funds. From Polynesia to California, songs of the surf have always found a good audience, perhaps because the sea itself is first and foremost a marvelous song.

7 | Science and Impermanence

To be objective is to treat the other like an object, like a dead body; it is to behave toward him like an undertaker.
—E. M. Cioran

Although human beings may not be perfection incarnate, they are the sole living beings who possess the ability to reflect upon their own activities, the only ones, in fact, who are concerned with the significance, the possible meaning of their existence.

The other mammals, from the great apes to the industrious ants, in spite of the cerebral capacities of the former and the social organization of the latter, are without any known inherited capability to engage in any sort of existential search. Thus animals, with the exception of human beings, are content just to be. Which is maybe not so dumb.

People sometimes question themselves to the point of becoming professional scholars and researchers. Those who ask questions about the practices and customs of the human race are grouped together in the disciplines of the humanities and social sciences. They are anthropologists, sociologists, philosophers, or psychologists. Surfing, for all the millennia of its past, is still a living, current practice, and it fascinates a few of these learned individuals. Some of them have the knack of seeing what is going on behind the diversion and recreation available on the waves, the tubes, and the tumbles. But you can never forget that their texts—like mine—are no more than collections of facts and interpretations and surely amount to no more than a subjective and limited vision. It is our way of participating in the development of a collective heritage that is always becoming deeper and richer. Perhaps one day the anxieties and concerns of reason in this endeavor of ours will make way for a blossoming of the full kind of knowledge, the mysterious connection that we sometimes recognize as intuition.

A Theme of Astonishing Power

There is no human activity that fails to deliver information about the meaning of life; but surfing, as the pure form of riding, is interesting for those prospecting for values because it is simultaneously a history and a living act. Because the first motivations for the activity appeared in prehistory and because it is still very much a contemporary experience, surfing seems to harbor within it an anthropological treasure horde that links the ephemeral to the perpetual.

As a tradition that lives on, surfing bears witness to a vision of human life that expresses astonishing harmony with the rhythm of nature, very much a theme in the postmodern period that the West is currently passing through. Surfing manifests this vision in the real world through the intermediary of an art in which force and elegance are united and the minuscule and the immense are reconciled:

> In a society in which everything is getting more and more complex, in which values are in the process of transforming and recomposing, in which order and disorder are intermingled, the symbolic figure of the surfer ceaselessly oscillating between balancing and falling appears as a theme of astonishing power.[55]

In order to convey to my readers the ideas that have taken the attention of researchers stimulated by this "theme of astonishing power," and thus to fill out the social portrait outlined in the preceding chapter, I have reviewed the principal works and scientific articles published on this subject.

The documents I have studied come mainly from the United States and France, with the exception of a master's thesis in anthropology I found at McGill University in Montreal. Commentaries by some authors who did not study surfing but who wrote on notions similar to those brought out by the other researchers I studied have also been included in this chapter, so as to enrich the subject and to make clear the universality that these scientific authors were trying to express.

Thinking Movement

It is important to stress that in studying surfing, one ends up directly studying something that is impermanent. The least one can say is that the terrain becomes somewhat slippery when you are obliged to deal with ideas such as change, the ephemeral, and movement.

So what can we say about research studies done on human groups that are in constant evolution? Because surfers, to avoid getting pinned down by mercantile or scholarly minds, opt for the strategy of change. This is the defense mechanism they adopt toward the mass media and its desire to co-opt the image of the surfer to sell cologne, for example, or an Internet service, or any other product that has no direct connection with surfing.[56] In fact it is enough to tell surfers they are surfers by virtue of a specific characteristic for them to change it.[57]

Of all the difficulties encountered in research in the human and social sciences, there is none greater than that of identifying elements, social or individual, that are not affected by the process of change. The very moment a context or an event is studied, that object of research gets busy changing. That is what we call social movement, natural evolution, the tendency of reality to become more complex. No matter—it is this same factor of change that results in something having one meaning today and the opposite meaning tomorrow, and in what appears as unity over here all of a sudden revealing itself over there as plurality progressing into the infinite.

Though surfers may be changing beings, balancing between two impressions, the researchers on their side are very inquisitive beings. They place their bets, when studying themes that are subject to the forces of change, on developing an understanding of the process by which things change.

Here we are dealing with an attitude in research that says that what is observable in social realities is observable in the form of flux. We are talking about an evolutionary social development marked by subjectivity, constructed with the help of very complex materials—the relations between various levels of reality.[58] Moreover, these materials (elements of reality) often differ in their form and content. Understanding the *process* thus makes it possible to interpret change dynamically rather than analyze consequences statically, taking a stance that is frozen in time and space.

Alternative Consciousness and Play

Alternative consciousness is the prevailing idea introduced by researchers trying to understand the motivation behind sports, such as surfing. The contemporary French sociologist Michel Maffesoli explicitly describes what I understand as the alternative consciousness when he discusses a new attitude that he defines as being attentive to the forces of the earth, to the vitality of nature:

> As an ideal type, it can allow us to distinguish what we might call ecological consciousness. This is a consciousness or sensibility that is heedful of what human existence has about it that is rooted, sensuous, corporeal.[59]

Thus the alternative consciousness expresses itself in opposition to a programmed world in which everyone is attuned to the same source of stimulation as their neighbors, convinced that they are individuals, whereas often they are no more than part of a complex system of consumption outside of which they are unable to exist, feel, and make decisions.

Jean Leloup, a Quebec rock singer with a couldn't-care-less attitude, whose relevance is inversely proportional to the seriousness of his self-presentation, sings that "advertising has transformed us." The alternative consciousness outright invites us to tune it out. It urges us to blow away mass conditioning the instant we make contact with ourselves, putting distance between us and the promises of a system that only too rarely lavishes caresses on us, as we are told by Antoine Maurice, the author of a book on surfing and political activism:

> Here we come back to the motif of personal development and the search for the self. For, whereas ecology retains a political purpose and places value on the classic notion of

political engagement, the alternative consciousness covers a larger territory. It also includes a nonpolitical field in which alternative lifestyles flourish. From new sports to therapeutic experiences, from macrobiotics to Zen. In this countercultural perspective of "do your thing," a shift has appeared: ever different promises of liberation are replaced by gratifications of immediate and fleeting pleasure.[60]

This sensibility, which engenders an alternative vision of the world, is animated by a spirit of play, and as Maurice points out, play here is not the opposite of seriousness.

As experienced in the universe of the ride, play carries the imprint of a search for freedom, expressed by the creation of a new order, an order that breaks free from the monotony of a linear and predictable life. We are talking about an activity that is "gratifying and psychologically absorbing, that is situated apart from ordinary life."[61]

According to Maurice, if you have to find an opposite for the concept of play, at the risk of "impoverishing the sense of it," it would be the norm, ordinary life, in short, habit. Play, in the context of the alternative consciousness, is thus not the opposite of that which is serious, because the alternative consciousness is itself, in some respects, very grave and serious in its tone and preoccupations:

> Serious because the entire ecological preoccupation . . . is imbued with a somber and weighty coloring. This generation of ecologists is carrying the weight of the world on its shoulders and it takes itself deadly seriously. Things only got worse after 1980, when the stream of ecology flowed into the river of pacifism.[62]

Thus the alternative-minded persons whose consciousness has been aroused, concerned by the fate of the human species, see the game as an experiment in taming new sensations that are a source of emotional entertainment. This also represents an opportunity to review the certainties that are supposed to constitute reality to see if they are appropriate to an individual or a collective. All of this leads Maurice to define this type of consciousness as "a game that consists in reforming, in a creative manner, the perception of an external reality."[63]

An amalgam of culture, psychology, and various social tendencies, the alternative consciousness expresses itself in a variety of ways in all strata of reality: on the individual and community levels as well as in political manifestations such as the Green Party.

Going beyond the form alternative consciousness first took in the crisis-awareness period of the 1970s and 1980s, different elements have characterized what is meant by *alternative*, especially elements that are play related—the throwing off of social constraints, the fabrication of conflicts, and an erratic and insatiable exploration of the field of the possible. This adventure on the fringes rewards the alternative person with the feeling of being someone who defines his or her own identity, a feeling of profound freedom.[64]

This analysis by Maurice, the author who has best defined the alternative character of the ride by connecting this attitude with various social events that have occurred in Europe and America, leads us in the direction of a process that he calls "a legitimization of the individual."[65] He sees this process as made possible by the alternative consciousness, which was itself called into existence as a reaction to conformism and the "massification" of societies. In this sense, the alternative consciousness is a way of searching for individual meaning in the face of the meaninglessness produced by societies subjected to the forces of uniformity.

The alternative consciousness does not purport to be able to create a new individual in the sense of a new superior category of human being. Rather it tends toward bringing back, whether intentionally or not, "old recipes as well as emerging values in mixing the dough from which the alternative individual is formed." This is not the approach of individualism, in which a person becomes part of a system where he or she works for personal profit, but rather an open door that can lead to the attainment of the full condition of individual, complete in itself and turned toward the world.

Individuation

The scientific literature about surfing, because the activity itself is unequivocally an individual one, takes great interest in the individual. An idea has been elaborated to mark the subtle distinction expressed by such authors as Maurice between the consciousness of self developed in the context of riding and egocentric individualism.

Surfers cultivate an acute awareness of the power of action through their relationship with nature, whose elements they use as a means of propulsion. This relationship with nature awakens them to the force of its elements yet does not push them to the point of idealizing a process seen as theirs alone. They are aware that there has to be, at least on an ecological level, a collaboration between the sea and the self. In short, it is not possible for the surfer to perceive the ocean merely as a material resource.

Jean-Pierre Augustin, who edited an anthology about surfing, effectively depicts a process that allows us to see a kind of individuation emerging that I personally describe as the consciousness of being part of a whole that is complete in itself:

> The basic experience of limits is also that of the basic irreducibility of the individual. Beyond a certain point, the ticket of collectivism is no longer valid. The waste of human beings and nature, the directionless drifting of the meaning of life, appears more inevitable in a society that exercises a monopoly of meaning. We should not expect to get out of this crisis without a minimum of cooperation and participation from individuals. Let us return to the individual his space of "personal development." Let us allow egoism to act within the confines of the inevitable so as to make it possible to build solidarities that are stronger because they have been freely committed to.[66]

The concept of individuation is linked to a movement with very old roots and it is making advances today as the result of a breakdown of the model of society in existence around 1960. This model, which has been described as holistic, promoted collective cohesion. Augustin stresses that this model "assigned to each person his status and role . . . [and] dictated behaviors and belief."

As a replacement for the holistic model, a society of individuation is emerging. Here it is no longer a question of the kind of individualism that is "a turning back on oneself" but rather of a phenomenon of individuation that pushes individuals to provide meaning to their own life.[67] It is a matter of waking up, of a consciousness that is on a higher level in relation to a power of action that is neither submerged in the conformism of individualism, which insidiously directs human beings toward standardized consumption, nor diluted within the context of a communism in which individual reflection quickly becomes incidental and empty. From the perspective of individuation, the human being is no longer the serf of an ideology or of capital and can be described by a new condition that I call individual sovereignty.

This all seems new and revolutionary, but it is in reality an ancient attitude that has been followed since time immemorial by the innumerable nomads who have roamed this earth. This idea is recalled by Maffesoli when he points out the great openness that one who is trying to know oneself has toward the Other:

> Thus the freedom of the wanderer is not that of the individual, who is frugal with himself and frugal with the world, but rather that of a person who is undertaking a mystical search for the "experience of being." This experience—and it is just for this reason that we can speak of mysticism here—is above all a community-related one. It always requires the help of the other. The other can be a small tribe that one belongs to or the great Other that is nature or thus and such a deity. . . . Thus it is nothing egoistic or turned back on itself but, on the contrary, the wind of the mind carrying along with it in its passage original anthropological values, and sowing in this way a sort of malaise in the breast of anyone who is trying to establish himself.[68]

Rejection of the Summons, Relic of Nomadism

In trying to define what they mean by rejecting the summons, some researchers, in addition to their extensive discussions of nomadism, make reference to a rejection of the sedentary and programmed life that is currently the norm in industrialized countries.

Gisèle de Lacroix and Olivier Bessy, two collaborators of Jean-Pierre Augustin's, speak of "the rejection of industrial society and its harmful environmental aspects." They state that the image of the surfer rejecting society, "turning his back" on it, comes

> in the literal sense from the fact that he is always looking at the sea, and in the figurative sense from his marginal lifestyle. [To be a surfer] means "going on the road," "chucking out everything" in order to take a one-way trip, fleeing civilization and its aberrations. Being "on the road" means signifying his rejection of current society.[69]

Radical surfers who are looking to escape from mainstream culture reject the limits and dangers proposed and imposed by modern society. They see something that's harmful to nature in the manifestation of our technocratic civilization. Remaining associated with the conventions that support it is a symbol of death for them. This being the case, there seems to be only one choice—to run away, to take a ride—in the direction of the absolute. Destination? Phantasmagoria par excellence. And if a surfer wants to desert a society that does not suit his or her values, the opposite turns out sometimes to be just as true—for the rolling stone, the one passing by, disturbs the one that remains in place:

There is no better way to describe the mistrust surrounding "migrating birds." For the philosopher who is seeking
to comfort the "Establishment" with its political power
and the social security it generates, the traveler represents
an undeniable moral risk, and this because he is the bearer
of new things![70]

On the Notion of the Natural Man and the Citizen

The fourth and last idea I have delineated—the idea that tries to tell
us that the surfer is a man of nature or a "noble savage"—is one expressed by nearly all the authors cited so far. To explain the duality
in play between the condition of the natural man and that of the
citizen, who could be better than the philosopher Jean-Jacques
Rousseau who, in *Émile*, points out that in preparing someone to be

a citizen, the person must be educated for the good of a cause other
than freedom:

> But what to do . . . when, instead of raising a man for
> himself, we want to raise him for the sake of others? In
> that case the combination is impossible. Forced to combat
> either nature or social institutions, we must choose
> between making a man and making a citizen—because one
> cannot do both at the same time.[71]

Further defining the person of nature, Rousseau, responding to
the passage above, goes so far as to define precisely the phenomenon
that Augustin calls individuation:

> The natural man is everything for him. He is the numeric
> unit, the entire absolute, which is related only to itself or

its like. The socialized man is no more than the fraction of a unit, which depends on its denominator and whose value lies in its relationship to the whole, which is the social body. Good social institutions are those that are best able to denature the human being, deprive him of his absolute existence and replace it with a relative one, and transport his "I" into the common, shared unity. Thus each individual no longer believes himself to be one by himself, but a part of the unity, and he is no longer responsive except as part of the whole.[72]

The Motivation

A breakaway, an escape from the world, absolutism—in these terms surfing appears to the average observer as a utopia. This vision that is cut off from reality, this position on the fringes, which at times seems to be possible only on another planet, cannot be demythologized except by confronting the question: What is the primary motivation for riding?

The motivation is to attain the state of hopupu. Without pretending to explain in detail just what this is, I invite the reader to explore with me in the next chapter a resource that is mysteriously refreshing.

8 | The Intuitive Search for Hopupu

> For a society to live or survive, it is necessary for something to exist alongside production and reproduction that is unproductive.
> —Michel Maffesoli, French sociologist

A Mysterious Gliding

> The experience of mystery is the most thrilling of all. It is the source of all real art and science.
> —Einstein

The afternoon is warm and humid, but a fresh breeze, full of communicative vitality, wafts gently through the leaves of a tree into Felix's hair. The boy is four years old. He is sitting on the back porch of my house. Now he jumps into my hammock and implores me to give him a board to assuage his need to ride, even though he is not yet coordinated enough to be able to stand all the time. "I want one of your skateboards, one of your boards so I can ride on my tummy."

I had made one to measure, just for him, a very little one, but the ones hanging on the walls of my apartment, the longboards, each one more attractive in its shape than the one before, are for Felix the real treasures in a changing world. It is he who is changing, getting bigger and ever more aware and conscious.

Thus, at the very moment when I am attacking the final chapter of this book, a child comes to see me so he can ride. A mysterious coincidence? It is an invitation, a break from work called up by my own desire to surf.

A few moments later, I find myself at the bottom of a slope full of curves that I have just drawn on the black and tarry coral of the town. The heat licks my whole body. I feel so light that I have become no more than a trace of adrenaline. I am full of joy, and my smile is big enough to burst my face. I am a king, I am a madman, I am completely hopupu.

The Relationship with Oneself

In certain [yoga] postures, especially when relaxing, it seems to me that I experience the same sensation as in the best moments of surfing.
—Yves Bessas, French surfer

What all human beings have in common, and yet strangely enough what also makes each of us a unique individual, is our relationship with ourselves—the discovery of each detail and its manifestations, at once multiple and universal, perceivable through the total experience of being.

When moving into the tube, impelled and enveloped by trance, no external thought can break in and distract the surfer without causing a fall, or at least a swerve. This is especially important if there happens to be a layer of coral beneath the wave.

In certain places there are no more than a few inches of water between the surfer's board and the razor-sharp ridges of the coral below. At the Pipeline, in Hawaii, Gerry Lopez's favorite surfing spot, the bottom is strewn with large growths of coral that create caves that can catch you or where you can get cut to shreds. No need to comment further on the fact that you need to clear your mind before letting yourself be seduced by a Pipeline tube, no matter how smooth and powerful it may be and no matter how beautifully it diffuses the light.

This process, this path of surfing, presents similarities with the paths of all people who have sought meaning and found their essence, whether through surfing, practicing zazen,[73] or studying the Tao, those whom the best-selling author Dan Millman calls "the peaceful warriors." Dominique Godrèche, a journalist who works with the Paris review *Psychologies*, expresses this idea clearly:

> For the Hawaiian champions, it is not only a physical
> performance but also formidable training in self-
> mastery, control of the emotions, and management
> of basic energy—*ha* in Hawaiian or *chi* in Chinese
> philosophy.[74]

Whether they refer to *chi* or *ki* or *prana*, all the warriors of planet Earth—the meaning of warrior is extended here to all those who consciously accept confrontation with the tragedy that life sometimes is—cultivate experiences that make it possible to opt in favor of the joy that fills us and empties us when we take pleasure in the simple fact of being alive, free from dwelling on life's absurdities.

Fundamental to surfers trying to become one with their own

nature, to unify their physical, spiritual, and mental dimensions, is that they must be capable of mastering the inner forces of being so as to tap into their source. Dig your heels in on the curve and chase time, point your nose, strike a proud figure, and spread your wings. Don't be anybody anymore, but feel, all at once, the whole that is in fact always already there, forgotten. Be a faucet of joy.

Joy

> Today we find that joy, just old-fashioned happiness, is one of the most essential elements of life.
>
> —Jacqueline Carol Marshall, educator

Guided by the vision of a wave, itself inspired by an undulation without significance for the average observer, surfers head off in a direction where only their senses can guide them. This is the direction of intuition, the sensation that enables us to understand the world and traces the route leading to the state of being called *hopupu*, in Hawaiian, or *stoked* in American English, the state that leaves our mouth agape and makes possible the appreciation of life at a high level. This is the sensory reward for having surfed well.

We are speaking here of a quest for the same sensation that children are seeking who let themselves roll down a steep hill or run until they have reached the point of exhaustion, shouting out cries of joy the whole while. They do that as they follow their minds down an imaginary path that is often circular.

The intuitive search for hopupu appeared to me as a kind of

138

off-road excursion—the road here being the progressivist and materialist vision of life today—a glide toward a region of being that is still natural but has gone missing. I read somewhere that balance is a synonym for freedom.

Epilogue

We are born to exist, not to know; to be, not to assert
ourselves.
                              —E. M. Cioran

*I*n following the way of surfing—and many other activities might
also have been chosen for this exploration—my intention was to
show that the experience of riding, because it requires a certain ac-
ceptance of the ephemeral, can lead to a greater knowledge of
human nature, and beyond that, of humanity's whole relationship to
its environment.

To begin with, in the first chapter I related the life experiences
that led me to become interested in surfing, then to the people who
practice surfing and to the values that are connected with this activity. Following the history of the Polynesians and continuing up to
that of the surfers of California, in the second chapter, it became
possible to see how the human visions of the world often structure
themselves around the activities engaged in by those who imagine
these visions.

Chapters three through six had the objective of doing justice to
the important imaginary dimension that is a characteristic of surfing,
an activity that is too often looked at purely in an athletic perspective.

Also present in this book has been the desire to highlight the
personal search for self-knowledge. I firmly believe that the ideas
presented in chapter 7, ideas having to do with the development of
an alternative consciousness that encourages the phenomenon of

individuation (that is to say, individual responsibility, not to be confused with contemplation of the navel), constitute a way, a path, that makes it possible to establish a basis for human activities expressed in the cultural, spiritual, and vocational diversity of the inhabitants of the earth.

Finally, it seemed to me important to recall that reality—for there is only one reality in which we are all evolving—exists first of all within the context of the path that we take in our effort to discover it. It is not in the destination but in the journey that the adventure is lived, as it is not by being a surfer but in surfing itself that it becomes possible to sense balance.

An Opening

If there is one question raised by reading about the history of surfing and by becoming aware of the values associated with it at the present time, it is surely that of knowing who we are individually and collectively and how that fits together with what really inspires us in life.

Too often we forget that we are living beings, vibrating in rhythm with a nature that has survived and will continue to endure far beyond any point we can imagine. Too often we accept having our lives set to the rhythm of office schedules. We orient ourselves by material and pecuniary concerns.

Surfing raises the possibility of an engagement with life that is occurring on a planet animated by a mysterious spirit that is strangely disposed toward nourishing us, surprising us by its complexity and dazzling us with its beauties. Formulated in the simplest possible terms, it is all about the present moment, the one we are in now and will be in perpetually.

Two elements are present in my questioning. Through its social environment, surfing displays the presence of commercial activity that makes use of the image of nature. From this point of view, it is a mirror that reflects the desire that some humans have to modify, re-organize, and turn a profit. Simultaneously, it is the expression of a dream sometimes forgotten, a dream of being in harmony with one's own nature, integrated into the First Principle that caused every-thing to emerge from the void, coherent and fulfilled. Surfing is a perfect illustration of two visions traditionally shared by human be-ings: the human being as a dominating figure, master of nature, ver-sus the human being who is reticent and restrained, integrated in the cosmos, and whose sole role is to be sure to preserve that which, among all things, keeps the universe in balance.

Without a doubt, surfing urgently forces the observer to con-sider, in this pivotal period in the history of humanity, reconnecting with nature; but from another point of view, it is legitimate for most of us to wonder if the surfer's way of life is not a bit too disengaged with regard to society, too bohemian for those who are caught up in the workings of the economic and political systems. I should recall here that it's not my intention to transform all my readers into surfers but to show what surfing can contribute toward enriching our thoughts, thoughts that have been impoverished in a world where everything is determined by the $acro$anct market.

Gliding in the Perpetual Present

Surfing made it possible for me to discover a flexible interpretation of the world and, through the practice of surfing and other arts of balance, I have been able to glimpse a universe that still illuminates me today. A universe that is strong in its connection to the present and to that which I can actually perceive.

From this state—the state of balance and consciousness in the present moment—a force springs that energizes and guides spontaneity and brings the greatest thoughts. They are the greatest, in my opinion, because they are pertinent, inspired by the situations that life presents. This fruition of balance, which makes it possible to grow in any direction without constraint, appears to me to be that which makes possible any form of art.

I am referring to a movement that allows one to complete or to further develop inspiring elements rather than pretend, in order to satisfy the ego, to create new ones, as Mr. Lee, controversial artist and avid devotee of Chinese kung fu, tells us:

> My task is simply to fill out the other half of the "unity"; my movement is Wu Wei (spontaneous act), which fits in with the circumstances and does so without prior preparation. The training of the mind and of the imagination, of the imagination and the Ch'i (breath), of the breath and the energy—all that has disappeared. There is no longer a goal to be realized. Everything flows from the source.[75]

In each moment, as in each wave and in each potential movement, I believe there exists an element of truth that can be expressed through a number of ways of being and acting that are in accord with the environment. These attitudes are natural and spontaneous in those people who have plunged into the present instant, who are attentive to the details of reality, who are first of all masters of their own ideas and then free in the actions that they decide to take. There is a genuine wisdom that lies within the power of people who master their actions and their thoughts. It is this same power that allows some of us to surf in a calm and balanced fashion, true to ourselves, independent of environmental conditions, on the water or in life in general, while certain others seem never to be able to reach this point and go so far as to persuade themselves that balance is not a part of their nature. The limits of these latter people—this has become more and more obvious to me—are often a reality only in their psyche. All their fears and ideas about misfortunes are quite often only eventualities, suggested possibilities.

Of course, many things do fall apart—our job comes to an end, or somebody betrays us—but what is all of that, right now, to the reality in which the strength of human beings is that they are animated by, and imbued with, a phenomenal capacity to imagine, to act, to receive, and to give?

There is no question of dogma here, because it is not necessary to believe in the spontaneity of the present and in the forces of balance—we are subject to them constantly, whether consciously or not.

There is no act of faith required; there is only a condition that it is necessary to accept, to which it is necessary to adapt. The present is the only dimension of time that is not imaginary. This is a state guided by the triumvirate of the "here," the "now," and the "like that." The first two ideas, the here and the now, have been developed at length by numerous authors and have been fully established; as for the "like that," it is to those occasions when one surprises oneself that I am referring here, those times when the action is not due to me or you but is a reality that has just happened—and there you go. It is the "it" of the beatnik, the spring that flows in the artist, the encouraging force that dwells in us when we act in a spontaneous way that leads to drawing the best from life as though it were a succession of waves that we catch because of a constantly aroused awareness, itself constantly being renewed through the fulfilling experience of the activity.

When freedom, or the choice of possible acts, remains an inflatable idea, far from what can really be observed, the imagination, the igniter of action, ceases to be useful because what it produces blocks the view: the dreams pass by and the dreamer is not ready. The obstacle here is the dreamer, because dreamers too rarely act from a perspective of freedom. In connection with this sort of idea, I would like to cite Arnaud Desjardins, a specialist on the living spiritualities of the East, a director of films on that subject, and the author of several works that touch upon concentration and the power of action:

> I dream about traveling. What can I do? I don't have a penny. I earn just barely enough to survive. I have nothing left over to take a long trip with. Okay, and if I were to travel, it would be useful to be able to get by in English, which is spoken throughout the whole world. As a result, I work on my English a bit. I haven't seen the Hindu Kush, or the Pamirs, or the Himalayas, or Burma, or Japan. I haven't stirred from my house, but I have acted and because of this very simple action, I am at peace.[76]

These thoughts might at first seem naive, but they are mind-boggling in their realism. Everyone is conscious of the present, and a great number of us content ourselves with that consciousness alone. Being conscious is in no way comparable to being really alive, to being coherent, to practicing the things that we fundamentally believe in.

Greed, coveting something, which is distinguished from dreaming in that it is a desire to possess rather than a motivation toward freedom or toward practicing an art, is one of the biggest wastes of energy that exist. To covet something instead of acting is like shrinking without ever bouncing back.

In any search we undertake, the content of what we experience does not matter very much. Isn't the essential thing that a person be completely involved in that searching process, so as to be able to react and move toward his or her own reality, in which, quietly, even the idea of freedom disappears?

Deconditioning, Exchanges, and Revolutions

Exploration, a task that is both awakening and entertaining, makes possible the discovery and expansion of knowledge. It illuminates the process of education, but at the same time it conceals within it an element of confusion.

New information, new conditions—no wave ever rolls in the same way again. Now to the left, now to the right, new vectors urging the mind to flee further and further in the same direction and to reflect on cohesion, to fit into the whole, to learn and to accommodate oneself to the idea that life is not a straight line.

Now to the left, now to the right. New vectors. Openings to the multidirectional reality of nature. This is what the practice of surfing and balance really has to teach: sometimes it is necessary to change the angle of attack, to accept letting the resource, a possibility, finally escape so that you yourself can disappear. Let a few blossoms of happiness get away from you with tears of joy emanating directly from the heart—send them off into the sky, without any expectations or premeditated intentions.

It is only a matter of letting the energy circulate in this micro-cosmic system that is the body, where the waves that start at the soles of the feet and rise up into your cheeks are free to make you smile and then fade away. Let go of the desire to keep the wave or the pleasure a prisoner. Stop having a view of the future in which there are only two eventualities, happiness and unhappiness. Learn to navigate with a 360-degree outlook; be ready to receive the impulse of whatever might come along. This is the ideal of the art of balance, a state of mind for those men and women who live in the magic that is in each moment of time. This state is called *astaticity*. It is a condi-tion of instability in which balance is perfect in all directions.

A theme that often crops up in my conversations with my bud-dies, when we are openly daydreaming about the accomplishments of people in their search for unity and coherence, has to do with syn-ergies in the fields of knowledge. By this I mean the coordinated ap-plication of many aspects of human knowledge to the actualization of integrated, all-embracing action. Exchanging and sharing among multiple processes, converging toward a balanced whole. The fruit of innumerable human experiences embodied in a raising of con-sciousness that would make it possible to attain what the biosphere already has—a state of balance that makes it so that the little ferns that die nourish the cedar tree. I am not talking about a political project or about the realization of an ideal that leads to some eccen-tric form of communism. I am speaking purely of the hope for a pro-cess of evolution that is in harmony with a present in which everyone knows what they are doing and what it is they want.

If in every revolutionary there were a complete revolution, exis-tence would be more complex and rich, more authentic and more dynamic, and much less energy would have to be wasted in creating conviction for a given future or in recalling the past. The present would be full, dense, and no one would any longer be hopelessly stuck in a narrow corner created by reason. Humanity would finally be able to project itself forward toward infinity with less anguish and anxiety, because once the conditioned path has been left behind, the possibilities become unlimited.

Before engaging in the practice of the present it is therefore necessary, I believe, to undergo a process of deconditioning, to come to understand through the experience of the quest for balance that the agitation of mental activity, the influence of others, and all the visions that we have, all exercise very powerful pressures that slow, divert, or prevent our actions.

To attempt to do what is not demanded, to make the effort to act and to build instead of simply reacting and then later grumbling about it . . . it is a matter of taking a journey, taking a break from the machinations of civilization, and returning with a self that has been forgotten, a new departure of the sort André Gide talked about at the beginning of the last century:

> While others were publishing and working, unlike them I
> spent three years traveling in order to forget everything I
> had learned in my head. This disinstruction was slow and
> difficult; it was more useful to me than all the instructions
> that had been imposed on me by men, and truly the
> beginning of an education.[77]

Clearly, in order to pass through our period in history and remain a little bit conscious, it is necessary to get completely away from the realm of the conditioned in order to see, from a distance, in what interest we are being asked to move forward. If there is a right or a responsibility that I hold to, it is that of being able to liberate myself, that is, to have the chance to explore my own capacities. And I think, as do many others, that it's impossible to arrive at this through the habit of the stupidly repeated action.

Cultivating Confidence

Regardless of the path one chooses in the search for balance, one should be encouraged if only because the search teaches us to live the glory of each moment, and because it helps those who experience it to become authentically themselves.

To place value on riding and finding balance in one's life and in one's surroundings is to accept change, to recognize the reality of an ephemeral world, and to be conscious of the only thing that exists and always will—change.

The challenge of adapting is usually more psychological than biological. In order to remain constant in a universe where everything is in flux, we need the kind of reliable confidence that stands up to the transitory nature of life, the confidence of someone who knows he or she is alive. The confidence of that comes from understanding and appreciating that impermanence has no dominion over the uniqueness of each moment.

The sensation of balance experienced by a young person skateboarding, by a painter moving about the picture she is working on, or by a dancer who gives his all for the pleasure of being alive for a moment—this is what builds that confidence. When the fear of falling disappears, one can imagine oneself riding, free from all hindrances. At that moment, life presents itself as a vast and inviting beach.

Glossary

When you know balance, you are not fascinated by anything;
you are not even attached to life, for you are life.
                    —E. M. Cioran

This glossary is in no way exhaustive and does not even pretend to
make a dent in the lexical universe of riding. It would be more appropriate to consider it a small tool that will help in understanding
this book.

air Synonym for loft or altitude. "He really caught some air."

boogie board or *body board* A small surfboard about sixty centimeters (two feet) in length that is ridden in the sphinx position,
that is, resting on the lower belly while raising the upper end of the
torso and the head, with arms extended. In France, the popular
term *biscotte* has the same meaning.

bottom turn A hard turn executed at the base of the wave that allows the surfer to stabilize speed. Speed is diminished in proportion
to the amount of surface of the board exposed to the resistance of
the water at the time of the turn. The bottom turn also makes it possible to climb back up toward the shoulder of the wave so the surfer
can execute maneuvers or take advantage again of the propulsive
power of the shoulder.

cutback A pivoting on the lip of the wave.

gremmie A beginner in surfing, awkward, inexperienced, who can easily cause accidents. "Nothing is worse than a gremmie out of control."

half-pipe Half-moon-shaped structure made of wood and sometimes covered with metal. Skateboard enthusiasts ride it like a molded wave.

hopupu Sublime state experienced by a person who has just become one with a wave. Ecstasy.

kinetic energy Energy in motion. In the context of surfing, this is energy made available as the wave breaks. It is this energy, caught by the surfer, that makes possible, among other things, the mysterious accelerations that characterize surfing.

lineup A spot offshore where the surfers line up to get a turn at a wave. Whether there is a line of surfers in this spot or not, it is still called the lineup, because the waves begin to curl there one after another.

localism Activity maintained by the locals at a surfing spot involving various techniques of dissuasion aimed at driving away or expelling strangers.

longboard Type of surfboard whose design favors catching small waves. The longboard is long and wide and has a rounded nose. The term is also used in referring to a long skateboard or a snowboard designed for use on powder.

pipe The inside curve of a wave when it curls into a tube.

pipeline A very long tube.

quiver Collection of surfboards of different shapes and lengths. Any experienced surfer owns a big quiver, which enables him or her to surf in a wide range of conditions.

rail slide Stylized move on a skateboard in which the skater rides along a structure that has a sharp or rounded corner (sidewalk curb or the lip of a concrete swimming pool). The weight rests on only the side rails of the board, the wheels do not touch the ground, and the board is in a perpendicular position to the rider's direction.

ride A person's movement on the board between the moment he stands up on it and the moment he falls.

rider Someone who uses a snowboard, skateboard, or surfboard.

shaper An artisan who makes surfboards, especially one who creates new forms and shapes.

spine This is a setup for skateboarding composed of two half-pipes side by side, together having the shape of a W. The spine makes possible particular maneuvers like jumping from one pipe to the other across the coping that separates them.

surf shop Shop where the equipment needed for surfing can be found. The surf shop is also a place where surfers meet.

tube The hollow tunnel formed when a wave breaks over itself.

waterman A man of the sea who excels in fishing (underwater fishing or any other kind), swimming, various kinds of boating, and sailing, as well as any other kind of aquatic activity that is available, such as surfing, sailboarding, kayaking, and so on. The waterman is also a master lifeguard.

zazen The form of meditation practiced in Zen.

Notes

1. This board was made to allow three surfers to take the same wave, to share a moment.
2. This site was named this way in reference to Pipeline, a legendary wave of Hawaii.
3. Thomas, Louis-Vincent, *Fantasmes au quotidien* (Paris: Librairie des Méridiens, 1984).
4. This dominant class held surfing sites protected by the threat of death. The members of this class were endowed with a superior physical constitution, resulting from the immigration of a specific group of Polynesians.
5. Gault-Williams, Malcolm, *Legendary Surfers: A Definitive History of Surfing's Culture and Heroes, Chapter Two* (serially self-published, 1997), p. 9.
6. Dixon, Peter L., *Men and Waves: a Treasury of Surfing* (New York: Coward-McCann, Inc., 1966), p. 22.
7. See chapter 5, Women Surfers.
8. Warshaw, Matt, "Paperweight: Matt Warshaw Looks at Surfing in the Mainstream Press," *The Surfer's Journal* 6 (1997): 3, 72.
9. Dixon, p. 27.
10. Ibid., pp. 28, 44.
11. Ibid., p. 42.
12. *Surfer's Journal* 6 (1997): 3, 75.
13. Bessas, Yves, *La glisse* (Paris: Arthème Fayard, 1982), p. 50.
14. Augustin, Jean Pierre, *Surf atlantique: les territoires de l'éphémère* (Talence, France: Éditions de la maison des sciences de l'homme d'Aquitaine, 1994), p. 29.
15. Bessas, p. 37.
16. Ibid., p. 40.
17. Ibid., p. 48.

18. Augustin, p. 37.

19. Mike Deffenderfer, master shaper and surfer of big waves of an earlier period; interview in *Surfer's Journal*, 1996, p. 31.

20. Loret, Alain, *Génération glisse: dans l'eau, l'air, la neige . . . la révolution du sport des "années fun"* (Paris: Éditions Autrement—Serie Mutations, number 155–156, 1995), p. 33.

21. Augustin, p. 223.

22. Loret, p. 222.

23. Ibid.

24. *Time*, Canadian edition, vol. 151, no. 12, March, 1998.

25. Ibid.

26. Thomas, p. 256.

27. Ibid.

28. Thomas, p. 255.

29. Loret, p. 199.

30. Ibid., p. 135.

31. Thomas, p. 238.

32. Bessas, pp. 98–99.

33. Chevalier, Jean, and Alain Gheerbrant, *Dictionnaire des symboles: mythes, rêves, coutumes, gestes, formes, figures, couleurs, nombres* (Paris: Éditions Robert Laffont/Jupiter, 1982), p. 888.

34. Thomas, p. 220.

35. Grof, Stanislav, and Joan Halifax, *The Human Encounter with Death* (New York: E.P. Dutton, 1977), pp. 125–127.

36. Prochasson, Bruno, "Surf et analyse sociale," *Surf atlantique: les territoires de l'éphémère* (Talence, France: Éditions de la maison des sciences de l'homme d'Aquitaine, 1994), p. 231.

37. Ibid., p. 233.

38. Maurice, Antoine, *Le Surfeur et le militant* (Paris: Autrement, 1987), p. 42.

39. *Time*, Canadian edition, June 1998, pp. 54–55.

40. This journal reference is lost.

41. George, Sam, in *Surfer*, May 1998, vol. 39, no. 5, p. 154.

42. *Time*.

43. *Surfer's Journal*, 1997, p. 78.

44. Suzuki, Daisetz T., *Studies in Zen* (New York: E.P. Dutton, 1963).

45. The Cajun who sings "working is too hard."

46. *Surfing*, July 1996, p. 54.

47. Godrèche, Dominique. "Le Surf: une discipline de l'esprit," *Psychologies* (Nov. 1996): 147, 59.

48. Kampion, Drew, and Bruce Brown, *Stoked: The History of Surfing* (Los Angeles: Taschen Verlag GmbH, 1998), p. 34.

49. Cited in Matt Warshaw, "Paperweight: Matt Warshaw Looks at Surfing in the Mainstream Press," *The Surfer's Journal* 6 (1997): 3, 76.

50. Morel, Alain, and Gilles Ouaki, *Tout sur le skateboard, Guide pratique Authier* (Paris: Éditions Guy Authier, 1978), p. 146.

51. Loret, p. 134.

52. Doudt, Kenny, "Rencontre avec un requin blanc," *Reader's Digest* (French language) (Sept. 1995), p. 74.

53. Soultrait, (de), Gibus, *Surf: L'homme et la vague* (Guéthary, France: Éditions Vent de terre/Surf session, 1995), p. 26.

54. Warshaw, p. 73.

55. Augustin, p. 19.

56. Wallace, Zane W., "Surfers of Southern California: Structures of Identity" (master's thesis, McGill University, 1992), p. 74.

57. Ibid., p. 71.

58. Laperrière, Anne, "Les critères des méthodes qualitatives," in Poupart, et al., eds., *La Recherche qualitative: Enjeux épistémologiques et méthodologiques* (Montreal: Gaetan Morin, 1997), pp. 366–377.

59. Maffesoli, Michel, *Du nomadisme: Vagabondages initiatiques* (Paris: Libraire générale francaise, 1997), p. 58.

60. Maurice, p. 47.

61. Ibid., p. 216.

62. Ibid., p. 52.

63. Ibid., p. 222.

64. Ibid., p. 53.

65. Ibid., p. 53.

66. Augustin, pp. 208–209.

67. Ibid., p. 17.

68. Maffesoli, pp. 64–65.

69. Lacroix (de), Gisèle and Olivier Bessy, "Glisse d'hier et surf d'aujourd'hui," in *Surf atlantique: les territoires de l'éphémère* (Talence, France: Éditions de la maison des sciences de l'homme d'Aquitaine, 1994), p. 19.

70. Maffesoli, p. 40.

71. Rousseau, Jean-Jacques, *Émile ou de l'éducation* (Paris: Garnier-Flammarion, 1966), p. 38.

72. Ibid., p. 39.

73. Zen meditation practice.

74. Godrèche, p. 56.

75. Lee, Bruce, *Chinese Gung Fu: The Philosophical Art of Self Defense* (Palm Coast, Fla.: Black Belt Communications, Inc., 1991), p. 17.

76. Desjardins, Arnaud, *Approches de la méditation* (Paris: La Table ronde, 1989), p. 60.

77. Gide, André, *Les Nourritures terrestres, suivi de les nouvelles nourritures* (Paris: Gallimard, 1992), p. 19.

Credits

Photographs on pages 60, 70, 90, and 140, © 2003 by Sebastien Larose.

Photograph on page 80, of Belen Connely in Costa Rica, © 2003 Debra Colvin of *Surf Life for Women*.

The photograph of the author on page 13 was taken by Joseph Arsenault.

All other photographs were taken by the author, © 2003 by Jean-Étienne Poirier.